WTF?! WOMAN TURNING F*FTY

Marga Ortigas has published several books with PRH SEA, including the critically acclaimed *The House on Calle Sombra*. She spent three decades travelling the world as a journalist, with a career spanning five continents and two of the largest international news networks. Along the way, she hit middle age and decided to step away from reporting the news before turning fifty. That shift in course led her back to her first love: writing.

A British Council Chevening Scholar, Ortigas earned her MA in literature and criticism at the University of Greenwich in the UK. She speaks three languages and writes as often as she can.

ALSO BY MARGA ORTIGAS

The House on Calle Sombra – A Parable (2021)
*There Are ~~No~~ Falling Stars in China (and Other Life
Lessons from a Recovering Journalist)* (2023)
God's Ashes (2024)

WTF?!

Woman Turning F*fty

POSTCARDS FROM A MIDLIFE 'CRISIS' . . . IN PROGRESS

MARGA ORTIGAS

PENGUIN BOOKS

An imprint of Penguin Random House

PENGUIN BOOKS

Penguin Books is an imprint of the Penguin Random House group of companies whose addresses can be found at global.penguinrandomhouse.com

Published by Penguin Random House SEA Pte Ltd
40 Penjuru Lane, #03-12, Block 2
Singapore 609216

First published in Penguin Books by Penguin Random House SEA 2025

Copyright © Marga Ortigas 2025

All rights reserved

10 9 8 7 6 5 4 3 2 1

ISBN 9789815144017

Typeset in Adobe Caslon Pro by MAP Systems, Bangalore, India

www.penguin.sg

Where there is ruin, there is hope for treasure.

—Rumi

Contents

'Tragedies', Torment, Thursdays

Fridays, Freedom, Finally

For You

Every beginning is a good one. Or so I tell myself. A new day, a new opportunity. A new year, a new adventure. A fresh start, a bumpy start—at least, it's *a start*. But not all beginnings are clearly defined. Not every start is marked by a whistle or a pistol. Many *commencements*, if not most, are lost in the mire of uncertainty. Occurring when we are too preoccupied with worry or fear to even notice. Like at a school graduation, which appropriately marks not just an end but also a beginning. One day we're hanging out with our friends griping over homework, then we blink, and suddenly, we've turned a corner. A new reality has emerged around us and we're adrift in the dander of the change. *How did we get here? When did this come about? Did dawn come and go without our seeing it? Were we asleep?* Perhaps. Or perhaps, just blinded. So used to focusing on our noses that we failed to feel the sunrise . . . the breeze caressing our skin . . . and the rain as it washed away the grime. Too shortsighted to see the panorama. We blink, and suddenly the days have spooled forward and we find ourselves *midlife*, which—though similarly terrifying—is a broader, gentler term than the less glamorous-sounding *middle-aged*. Besides, one can be mid-life, in a sense, and not be chronologically at the midpoint of their existence.

Well, I blinked and, poof, I was done with my thirties. They went by so fast I am still suffering from the whiplash. That was it, right? That meant I was officially entering *midlife?* The stage at which according to the prevailing notion I'm supposed to go into *crisis*? Or was that solely the privilege of men? When they can do things that are seemingly 'out of character' and get excused for it? I wasn't sure.

According to stereotype, midlife is when people *reassess* (there's that word again) where they're at in their lives and make necessary changes. Divorce figures rise, there are sudden migrations to lands of 'better opportunity', and unexpected shifts in career. A life purpose or two might even be 'discovered'. At least, this is what we were shown on TV—think *Dynasty*, *thirtysomething*, and *Knots Landing*, to name a few examples. And because I saw it on screen, I could recognize it in a few acquaintances and neighbours. Like a virus or a disease that one had best avoid.

I don't, however, recall my mother going through such a critical, colourful period of 'lunacy'. She didn't suddenly change her hairstyle or buy a sports car and indulge in useless luxury items. Nor did she *trade things in* for younger, brighter models or walk out of a job just because. To be fair, I don't recall my father doing any of that either. Does that mean this midlife phase so oft referenced in popular culture isn't real? Or limited in whom it affects? If it doesn't *afflict* everyone, would *I* be free of it?

When I was in my teens, I could barely imagine being twenty-nine. The age was so far off it was in a new millennium. *A new millennium!* That was mind blowing for an analogue child like me. But then I blinked, and blinking again, I found myself in my fourth decade, completely at a loss as to *how* I got there. Shouldn't extraordinary things have happened to me by then? Shouldn't I have all the answers required to manoeuvre through life with certainty? So how come I felt no different to who I was at twenty-three? I definitely didn't feel like an adult. When I was growing up, forty was the age of an A. D. U. L. T.— and that's how I still see it. If you're forty, you're *old*. (Ahem, there's *that* word again.) Thing is, I still can't believe I've long since jumped through that hoop.

My relationship with age is a strange one. When I was nineteen, I was presenting the evening news for a national broadcaster. An unusual and unexpected position. The network did all it could to make me appear older—shoulder pads, hair spray, big earrings, tailored suits—but I still just looked like a college student dressed in her grandma's clothing. Cosplaying. Why was I performing such an adult task as delivering the news? I have absolutely no idea. Cheap labour? I have since asked my ex-boss that question and even on retrospect, he didn't have much of an answer. I had gone in for a part-time job while in college and the network put me on air. Go figure. The point is, I was always chronologically younger than the age I was meant to project. But when that projected age crept up on me, I found myself desperate to hold on to the youth I had long tried to hide.

And now, here we are. I'm three decades into an unplanned career in journalism, analogue has all but given up the ghost, and though there have been few surprises in terms of technological advancements—(What? I watch *Star Trek*)—people and society these days aren't anything like I imagined at the turn of the millennium. What happened to the dreams of a kinder world? Where is the Utopia we were meant to be approaching? Perhaps humanity in general is in the midst of a crisis. Could it be that we as a civilization are entering a period of midlife? A time in which we reflect and ponder the existential questions: *Who are we? Why are we here? Who else is here with us? What is the point of it all?* It would not be the first time in human history. Through every age and cycle of renewal, there are those who would guide the way. As many wars as we continue to fight, there are also teachers of light. And as vengeful as those in power might get, there are also peacemakers among us. But I suppose not enough yet to completely dissipate the dark.

So this is where you find me. Grappling with the light and shadows of my journey thus far. An examination prompted by changes beyond my control. Physical, physiological, and social. I was needing to flee and find an alternative to the reality that shackled me. Needing to breathe after holding my breath for so long. I am sure there are those of you who know exactly what I mean. (Fancy seeing you here!)

Most books on the subject will tell you midlife ranges from the age of forty to around sixty-five, but that doesn't mean you can't feel the 'midlife malaise' earlier. Or indeed, later. It can come during any period of transition. The loss of a job, a change in status, getting diagnosed with an ailment, or a loved one's passing. It can come when you go from being in the prime of youth to . . . no longer being at that stage. And while it certainly doesn't require a clinical evaluation, the *symptoms* of midlife—dissatisfaction, anxiety, and self-doubt among them—have been greatly researched and detailed. They add up to a rather troublesome, turbulent time. A period when things are topsy-turvy and you're in turmoil, desperately searching for equilibrium. Worse, it's a period in one's life that doesn't necessarily have a start date nor a predictable end. How I wish I could tell you this book would give you answers where you might have questions, but I fear it may just raise more queries.

So, hello. And welcome to this midlife pondering. We haven't been formally introduced, and though we may never meet off the page, I am so very glad you've picked up this book. I won't pretend to know why, but I am grateful you did. Maybe, like me, you are *mid*-life—for any variety of reasons—and in search of peers. Or, maybe, you're just curious. Whatever the reason, I hope you stick around. Please know that this in no way is going to be a scientific exploration of a typical or natural human experience, nor is it a journalistic investigation. All this aims to do is add to the record of personal narratives that contribute to the public conversation around midlife—gosh, what a seemingly finite word—that though it might not seem obvious, does in some way afflict us all. We all inevitably face moments of transition. Such *movement,* such inconstancy, is part and parcel of living. We can opt to flow with the tides of change or fight against them. Some of us may be able to take a moment to reorient ourselves and catch our breath, but there are those unable to allow themselves that same experience. I cannot overlook the millions of people with more pressing matters to contend with, tangible, material concerns that prevent them from looking at what's immaterial and *in*tangible. But this . . . this . . . existential 'crisis' should not also be dismissed as a mere frivolity as it's a very real undertaking for quite a multitude, affecting their choices and their manner of *being*, of how they move through the world.

So if you count yourself among those *adrift* and are in want of company, make yourself some tea, find a spot of sunlight, and peruse a chapter. These pages are not meant to be read in a single sitting, take your time, take a pause, and here we go.

Having said this, please, do forgive the self-indulgence of this exercise.

BIG QUESTION #263

AM I HAPPY?

aka

What the heck is going on with me?

Alarm Bells

Adele used to yell at me when the sun rose. Yes, that Adele. One of her songs was my alarm/ringtone—I know, trite. But can you guess which one? Anyway, it was an attempt to give myself a soothing start to the day . . . before my news editor rang and inevitably ruined it.

After a few weeks, the song/ringtone became so irritating that I wanted to throw my mobile across the room whenever it sounded—because it let me know that somewhere around me something horrid was happening and I would have to go report on it. Mind you, that never used to be my response to a work call, but something had clearly snapped. I was in my forties, living out of a suitcase, and my body had not healed from several traumas. (Vehicular accidents while travelling for work that resulted in multiple neck injuries.) They slapped a neck brace on me in Japan once—and Bob's your uncle—I thought I was good as new. I was wrong. I am still getting weekly treatments for it now—it's been a decade since the last injury.

Again, I digress.

I was so lucky to be doing work I loved—and I mean LOVED. I got to go places, see all sorts of things, and meet people in the most extraordinary of circumstances—(and I won't say 'amazing people' because I believe all people are amazing, full stop).

I travelled across Europe, covered the Middle East, and most of Asia. I even got to report from Oceania. Most people have not even heard of Yap!

But it got so the world squashed me under its wheels. I tried to keep pace, but it took me under. There were days I would wake up in the middle of the night and not remember where I was. Hotel rooms all began to look the same, and the staff in several places knew me by name. There was even a time I had to report on three different stories from the one location in a single day. Within the same hour! The cameraman just angled his shots—from the same spot—to appear relevant to each of the stories.

Eventually, not only was my body unable to cope with the lack of sleep and constant movement—the pain got so I could no longer trek up mountains, ride outriggers in choppy waters, or perch on the back of trucks driving down dirt paths the way I used to, all of which were practically part of the job description—but worse, the fire in my spirit had gone out. I began to feel like a zombie. An automaton who could regurgitate copy and headlines because it all began to feel like a cycle. Same story, different location. Sometimes, it was the same location, same story—simply different characters. Or sometimes, the same characters, at different stages of life. The cameraman and I fell into a routine. Geopolitical strife? We had analysts on speed dial and accessible government spokespeople on text terms. Super typhoons and floods? We knew where to go for the most devastating shots and who to look for in a community to get the most moving stories. It became rote. And the news—human tragedy—should never be rote. It is an injustice to treat it as such.

Then, my parents passed away. Both from illnesses, several years apart. And both at times of great news headlines that also had me frayed. I knew it was bad when just weeks after my mother died, I was speaking to a newly orphaned fourteen-year-old who had lost everything in a super typhoon and we were both crying so much I had to ask the cameraman to stop recording. I did the young boy an injustice by clouding his pain with my own. I knew then it was time to take a pause.

Waters were flowing too quickly for me to keep afloat without straining to paddle. I feared not only being pulled under but dragging others down in my wake.

I had to breathe, rest my body, and recharge. I had to deal with things left undealt with and grieve. I had to find a way to comprehend all that I had witnessed and experienced. But I didn't listen to myself then and kept going for another couple of years.

Now that I have finally taken a step back, I know how fortunate I am to have been able to get off that hamster wheel. But I am also haunted by the fear that I have abandoned my calling.

That Adele song: 'Water Under the Bridge'.

One and Done, aka Over It

It was around one in the morning when I knew, in my gut, I was done. Why do I recall the exact time? Because a new president had just been elected in the Philippines, and I was wrapping up my final live report on it for the international news channel I worked for. It had been a long week, a long month, a long year—as they always were—leading up to that moment. Ceaseless days of newsgathering, producing, and travelling, weeks upon weeks on end, months turning into years rolling into more, seemingly without pause or rest. Our news crew was going from earthquakes to super typhoons to landslides. Conflict zones, humanitarian crises, and political upheavals. There were several viral outbreaks and a nuclear disaster. Everything short of Armageddon. Birthdays passed without being marked and 'personal' lives were an afterthought. Personally, I felt like a sieve through which the world and all its madness passed. Barely able to contain my *self*. But it didn't matter—or so I told myself—it was part of the job. It was our *duty* as journalists to set aside our emotions. We *owed* it to the people we covered and those who watched from home. Journalists are meant to be a funnel and a platform. There to aid those unable to speak for themselves. In such profound whirlpools of human experience, it is easy to lose sight of your core. And without a centre, I began to feel . . . translucent. Like I wasn't *real* or solid, not rooted or grounded in the tangible world. I suppose you could say I felt like a zombie.

Neither here nor there. Trapped somewhere in between. And the more happened around me, the less I felt like a person.

For years, I carried on as if I were nothing more than a blank screen that reflected other people's realities. And I was okay with that because it kept me from having to look at my own. But then, as it does, what was going on in my own metaphorical backyard became impossible to overlook. Things at home were literally breaking down and in need of fixing. Appliances were conking out, pipes were clogging, and family members were falling ill. But I carried on working through it all as best I could, until the sound of my morning alarm began to fill me with anxiety. Until I started to dread the ring of the phone. Until the voice of my editor felt like Satan's call. Natural calamities began to all feel the same, and I struggled to keep a sombre expression while covering an impoverished nation's corrupted elections.

It was 1 a.m., I was in Manila, and I had had enough. I knew then I couldn't go on as I had been. I was exhausted, I was numb, I felt empty. I had no more words left to share with a viewing audience. I couldn't think, and I could no longer see straight. My mind had stalled, and I just wanted to get off the ride. Mornings were hardest of all. I no longer had the drive to get up and greet another day of work. Even if those extraordinarily diverse and unpredictable workdays had fuelled me for decades. It was dawning on me that I had reached my breaking point. I realized that I had left my thirties behind and my life was not anything I had imagined. I was plagued by migraines, suffered endless back pain, and my knees were beginning to feel unstable. I seemed to be losing my focus and felt like I was growing unable to hold my balance.

So, without much more consideration, I called a time out. I had to. It felt like the wise thing to do. It was what I owed the job. Yes, can you believe it? I was still thinking about the *bloody job!* Since I could no longer engage with the demands of the profession as expected, I thought it would be best if I took a break. Yes, a break. That's all I was planning on. A few months. Maybe a year? At this point, I had been working in news for more than two decades—so this *break* was going to serve as a palate cleanser. Like the few years I took in my twenties to complete my master's. It would be a long soak in a bath after a difficult journey through the woods. Yes, after that stomach-turning election victory of yet another self-serving politician, I decided to just stop.

Then, what? Frankly, looking back now, I no longer remember. I think I cut myself off from social media—all media really—and went on a trip. I took long scenic drives, enjoyed easy visits with faraway friends and family, and slept a lot. Or at least I tried to. I tried to read and watch films—but nothing could hold my attention. It seemed my brain just wanted to switch off. Basically, I think I took about a month or two just to do *nothing*. And then, true to form, I went back to *needing* a reason to get up in the morning. I mean, what was I *doing* in all that nothing? And who the heck did I think I was *not working?* OMG—I was not working! How the heck was I going to support myself? I needed a salary! My savings were only going to get me so far—and that 'so far' was seeming closer and closer. I began to panic. In a way I hadn't before.

When my parents were alive, I had somehow subconsciously seen them as a security blanket. I could take risks—or rather, not *consider* anything too risky—because I was confident that if things went awry, I could 'go home'. I could go home and be safe. But my parents had both passed by this time, and I had nothing to really fall back on. There was no 'going home' other than to the darkness of my own numb and empty soul. (Yes, things at times felt that bleak.) Good grief, what was this melodramatic melancholy? It was so . . . uninspired. Uninspiring, and certainly unoriginal. Wait, was this—gulp, dare I say it?—a *midlife* crisis?

I seemed to be ahead of my peers. Around me, people my age were still thriving in their chosen fields, while I had grown tired of what I thought was my life's purpose. My 'dream come true'. How'd I get to 'crisis' point so quickly? Although I was older, I didn't feel a day past twenty-four. But then again, I also felt rather ancient. Like I had been doing this forever and a day. So, I decided to pause—without a prospect or a plan—and promptly realized that I was lost.

'Why don't you podcast?' said a friend and former colleague who's a generation younger. She uttered something about overhearing the 'engaging' conversations I had with others my age and how interesting it might be to record us as we discussed getting older. Buttering me up further, she said there was even a term for people like us who seemed to transcend the boundaries of our generation and remain engaged with the world—*perennials*. Coined by American entrepreneur Gina Pell to describe those who 'stay current with technology, and have friends of all ages'. I liked the sound of that. Perennials.

'Think of it like you're exploring being in transition,' my friend and former colleague said. 'You're just going from one aspect of your life to another . . . and age, age is just a number . . .'

Right. A cliché . . . but perhaps also true. Growing older didn't have to mean growing old. An ending is also a beginning. Nothing has to be so finite. And I did always feel better when I thought I was working towards something, so maybe this podcasting would give me a deeper goal.

'You're used to interviewing all sorts of people, exploring different perspectives and getting to the truth of things,' the younger ex-colleague continued, 'maybe you can do the same for yourself?'

And so, I did. Believing that preparing the podcast would also help me feel less adrift. Which it accomplished . . . and I also picked up a new skill. Producing and editing a podcast. The show was a great excuse to ask people—sometimes complete strangers—potentially intrusive questions. Potentially intrusive, but infinitely enlightening. Every episode, we discussed a particular transition—from gangster to social worker, from journalist to farmer, from rockstar to dad. We looked at how to tackle life changes and get through the uncertainties of being 'in crisis'. True to its theme, the podcast, called *About That*, has also been reinvented several times and is now in its fourth season. Somehow, I trust it is reaching the listeners it needs to. Across generations.

Considering the number of books on the topic that are now popping up on my social media feeds, I realize I am not the only one who has tried to make sense of the niggly 'midlife' feeling inside by looking externally, by asking others if they ever felt the same. And if they did, to share how they survived it. After everything I've read and from the people I spoke to, one thought came through clearly: things happen as they happen and you will somehow find it in you to adjust. Make plans for the future to revive your interest in life . . . and when you feel like all is lost, by all means, find yourself another dream.

Find another dream. How I held on to that line. I had heard it in a historical biopic, *Ignacio de Loyola*, titled after its lead character, a sixteenth century soldier who was constantly beset by obstacles. At the end of the film, after a grave injury made his ultimate dream of military glory unreachable, instead of being defeated, Ignacio walked down a different road saying, 'It's just time to find another dream.' He went on to teach and establish a religious order—the Society of Jesus—that has become one of the most influential in the world.

Another dream. My life wasn't over just because I gave up my job, so why was I going to let the darkness win? That's when I began to write a novel. It was a childhood dream long set aside. The way I saw it, writing news reports was stitching together a tapestry from threads that were provided by a master weaver. I could disappear in someone else's poetry. But this—my own novel—was entirely another matter. Putting together 100,000 words held no comparison to a TV news script that was barely a page long. And with nothing able to hold my attention at the time, I was worried I would fail at this book thing before I could even start.

Could I do it? Write long form? String together 100,000 words? With nothing left to lose, I just jumped in, deciding to *lose* myself in written language. I gave myself over to the word because the world around no longer held any interest. I looked outside—and was just completely over it.

RANDOM NOTE

The thing about stories—they give us the illusion that life and events have form and meaning.

*No clue where I got this. I had scribbled it among my notes.
11 September 2019

3·19 a·m·

Every morning—if it can even be called that considering the charcoal darkness outside—I get up at this time for no real reason. My neck hurts. My back is tweaked. My bladder, not too full. In short, nothing extraordinary enough to rouse me. But something somewhere in the ethers of the Universe pokes me awake anyway, and I open my eyes to a general sense of unease. Not dread or fear or anxiety. Just . . . unease. For no reason that is clear to me at 3-freakin'-19 in the morning.

Three-bloody-nineteen.

Every freakin' day.

You would think there was some numerological relevance to the time—at least, I did after the first several days of finding myself awake at that precise minute. But no. Apparently not. I checked. As one does when one finds something in their lives that they can't make sense of. They trawl through the endless mine pit that is the interweb, searching for answers to their mundane, morose discomforts. Trust me, I have investigated most everything. Chakras. Gong baths. Crystals. Angel readings. Psychotherapy. Meditation. Spiritual cleansing. Aural or energy shifts. Astrology. Astronomy. Neurotheosophy. (Yes, I did make that last one up—but sounds plausible, right?)

Anyway, I have looked up all sorts of things—is all I am trying to say—and there is no explanation for the general malaise that wakes me up mid-pre-dawn-morning. (And there is that word again—*malaise*.)

'Must be peri,' a friend who shall remain unnamed dared say as we discussed this phenomenon one gin night or two ago. I laughed—is she kidding? Ridiculous.

Me? *Peri*-menopausal? I hadn't even heard that word before. I mean, not really. Sure, it was beginning to be whispered about in some of my circles—but who knew what it really meant? *Perimenopause?* I gawped at my friend. No way. Not me. Not a chance in he—

'Hang on,' said my doctor a few weeks later when I made the mistake of mentioning it. 'She may not be wrong.'

I would like to say I stopped going to that doctor—but that would just be silly.

So, here I am, at 3.19 in the morning, writing this to tell you my neck is fine because I took a pain pill before going to bed. My back is—meh. And my bladder is under control. But feck it all to heck if I didn't wake up again for no *goddang* reason at bloody 3.19 in the morning!

I know I am not alone—the aforementioned nameless friend is ranting endlessly in one of our instant messaging app chat groups about some news programme she is watching at this hour, and I see locals on social media pinging inexhaustible notifications. Hello, mid-pre-dawn companions!

I wonder though if I am the only one feeling hot at this hour despite the air-conditioning. Must be global warming. These old ACs just can't cope with the rising heat. I must get it checked in the morning—the AC, not global warming. Sorry, the condition of my appliances is not relevant to you—just a side note to remind myself in a few hours, when the sun is up, to call the repair guy. Yes, my memory is not what it used to be either. Sometimes I swipe on the food delivery app to place an order for pizza having forgotten I just had lunch.

I digress.

Where was I? I didn't have this much trouble focusing—or sleeping—when I was working . . .

Dang it. It's now 3.40 a.m. Where did the twenty minutes between the previous sentence and this one go? Oh yes, I got up and went to the bathroom. Decided to tweeze my brows. I can feel them growing despite what the mirror might tell me in the light of day.

No, I do not suddenly have hair above my lip. And for the last time, I am not perimenopausal!

Perimenopause means 'around menopause' and refers to the time during which your body makes the natural transition to menopause, marking the end of the reproductive years. Perimenopause is also called the menopausal transition.

—Mayo Clinic

*Why does this say 'your'? As if presuming that only women will search for what this is online. What does that say about the state of healthcare?

Dear reader,

This is not a book about perimenopause. Just reiterating.

Thank you.

—The author

Sleepless In · · · Where Am I?

If I am honest, I think I left journalism so I could sleep. And yet, here I am, nearly six years from the job and I can't remember the last time I slept through the night. *WTF*. And let me tell you, I am exhausted. I know I am not the only one my age who feels like this. I am surely not the only woman. You will sometimes spot us sitting together mid-morning and bitching—I mean, brunching—in a nearby bistro. We'll likely be wearing shades to cover our eye-bags and sipping our flat whites or iced teas while picking at our egg white omelettes and secretly wanting that slice of cake. We'll not have slept the night before and be talking about our uncomfortable pillows or our lack of exercise while unmindful of our poor posture. This newly sedentary lifestyle is doing me in.

I never used to 'brunch' before. I never had the time. When I was working, I was *working*. So, I focused on work, and everything else fell by the wayside. Was that a healthy way to live? Oh heck no. I get that now, but it was what it was. And you can convince yourself of anything. So, I convinced myself that I was doing the right thing by focusing on work and doing what mattered. And back then, I seemed able to sleep anywhere. We (the news crew) slept (i.e., took naps) in the back of cars next to graves, along roadsides, in roofless rooms during a thunderstorm, and crammed together—unwashed and unfed— in a bamboo hut. There were days I moved around so much I didn't even know where I was. I would wake up in one country and go to bed in another. But no matter how frenetic the pace,

I could sleep, and upon waking, not feel like the undead. Not a zombie. Nor an automaton. Now, that seems to be my regular state. As if all the frenzied activity has finally caught up with me. I am just so existentially exhausted that there are days I do not want to move at all. And that just invites more melancholy. It's a cycle I am not thrilled to partake in.

So . . . what to do? I have read the self-help guides and seen all the memes online from the self-styled gurus. I know I have to exercise, eat a balanced diet, and work on my core strength. But that entails having a vision of tomorrow that I currently don't possess. When I think of the future, all I see is black, like a deep ravine or a massive cinema after the day's last showing. Hollow and dull. This is not to say I do not believe in an afterlife, just that I seem to have lost the spark, the desire for . . . anything. And I think it's when we no longer want or yearn for something, even if it is simply peace of mind, that we lose what spurs us on. That impetus we need to carry on. Why get up in the morning? Sometimes, I admit, I ask myself the question. It's a selfish one, I know.

With my days now more fluid and freer than I was used to, I actually have more time to sleep, but despite all efforts, I remain awake. Exhausted, but conscious. Often held hostage by a parade of anxieties marching before me like manic sheep endlessly bounding over a fence. Where do I begin to unpack each one? The absence of a steady job? Not having a plan? Lacking a dream? All of that rolled into one? Maybe I also feel I have nothing *substantial* to do? And though that might mean more time to brunch, there are fewer people I want to brunch with. I am careful now about who I spend time with. And I also feel too tired for polite conversation. Why bother? Though most of my friends are unmarried, we're all in a similar 'non-sociable' state. Preferring to hibernate unless in the right frame of mind. Some don't even answer their phones and need to space out the social events they attend. To 'cleanse' herself of any picked up negative energies, one friend put it. Understandably. A 'detox' of sorts. It does take it out of you to be around so many people.

How did a piece about sleep become about socials? (For post Gen-Xers, that would be social gatherings, not social media.) When I was younger, we could go on for days in a cycle of partying and work, with sleep almost an afterthought to the rhythm. I think I remember burning with so much *life* then that I just kept wanting to blaze a path where the fire flowed. Now, just writing that sentence winded me. The energy it took to even think it has me spent and drained. And have I mentioned how I yearn for sleep? That is all I seem to want, but it has eluded me for going on . . . oh, six years? Maybe it's been longer? I don't even know. All these endless days just seem to bleed into the next. With no spark, no fire, no colourful splotches . . . Just an unwashed blanket of grey suffocating any peace I have been longing to claim.

It has been a *LONG* metaphorical winter's night and I am cold. I feel . . . nothing . . . but the chill deep within my bones. And everything, *everything*, makes me want to cry . . . over its incapacity to make me even want to burn. I look out the window on this skyless morning, where smog has draped itself over the crowded city. Nothing seems to move, nothing calls to me, there is nothing of interest . . . I just want to draw the blinds and shut my eyes to the ache inside.

Someone calls for brunch, which I dare to turn down. I have more than enough company this muted morning with my sleepless melancholy.

Alphabet Soup

I don't know about you but there are days when I can barely bring myself to handle a sentence. I mean that literally. I can't read—it's too invasive. (Imagine, someone else's thoughts *inserting* themselves in your mental space?) I can't watch TV—it's too noisy. All that flashing technicolour and booming sound. I can't even listen to an audio book—again, too psychically intrusive.

As it is, I feel like I am swimming around in a nebulous bowl of cloudy, tepid alphabet soup. Unable to fish out any letters or see them clearly. And words are the most basic building block of our thoughts. So, on days like these, I end up feeling like I am submerged in formless *blah*. Yes, blah. (I know I said bleh elsewhere in this book, well, that's different.)

So, now, blah. That is the most I can commit to. I can't even say there are emotions. Surely, emotions have some sort of skeleton. Some semblance of an underlying structure. But this … *malaise*—for want of another w-o-r-d—this … soup … feels like a stupor. Like being numbed by nothingness. And on days like this one, I just want to curl into a ball and bawl. I can't even phone a friend. That would entail having to speak—and like I just intimated, on days like this one, my best friend in the world, my words, this language, they fail me.

WHAT IS THE POINT OF IT ALL?

Duster Diary

There's a place in the mall that you can bring your clothes to when they need mending. If only such a place existed for our souls. Oh. I forgot. That's what church is for, no? Religion? The opiate of the masses and all that? So, how's your opium going for you these days? Me, it's like I quit smoking—but in the opposite way to going cold turkey.

I've found that people's relationship with faith and a deity evolves throughout their life. That's if they have any relationship at all with such a celestial concept. Many learn or take on the beliefs of their families—or respond to what they're taught at home by choosing to negate it. It's what children do. No? I've encountered many an atheist descended from the most devout and some of the most devout born from those who didn't believe in anything they could not see. Then there are those who pick things up on their own. One way or another, we all have some sort of relationship to or opinion on the supernatural. The way we might with chocolate.

I was once told about a man who was raised a Protestant then became an atheist when he reached adulthood. On his deathbed decades later, he supposedly asked to be baptized Catholic. Not long after that, he peacefully left this mortal coil. This was told to me as a lesson in faith. The moral being that since I was raised a *believer*, I should 'stay in the lane', as it were, and save myself the trouble of 'going rogue' only to, at the end, look to amend the 'error'. But what then of the adventure in between? I am kidding. Only just.

It's a deeply personal thing, faith. And as much as I understand the power of sharing it with a community, there's also something to be said about keeping it private. I feel the same way about opinions. There better be a darned good reason you are not keeping those to yourself. Especially if you're a working journalist. But this is not a point to be made here.

Let's get back to darning, which is why I started writing this in the first place. I took some items to be darned at the mall. A well-worn T-shirt, a pair of trousers that needed to be hemmed, and a duster. Which to me, was the most important item of all. For the uninitiated, when I say *duster*, I do not mean a piece of cloth—i.e., a rag—that is used for wiping dust particles off surfaces. Nor do I mean a large, shapeless muumuu of Polynesian origins. It is not a caftan either—those tunics are often sashed or belted, go down to your ankles, and have sleeves. Rather constricting, if you ask me, and the total opposite of the dear duster I took to be darned. A billowy, cotton 'dress' for lazing at home, the duster went just past the knees, had pockets, and a delicate, crocheted neckline. It was so worn, several patches were already sewn onto it to keep it from becoming more frayed.

'This'll cost you,' the lovely seamstress said upon inspection of the latest hole. 'You're better off just getting a new one at the bargain market,' she offered as if I wouldn't know. 'They're crammed full of this stuff—for half the price of the mending.'

I had been expecting the comment. I'd heard it before. It was repeated every time I took a duster to be darned. Usually, it was accompanied by surprise that someone my age would wear such an item, since it was seen as an 'old person' thing.

'It's my mom's,' I whispered conspiratorially. 'You know how they get . . .' I added an eyeroll to make my point.

'Ay sus!' the woman laughed, 'Why didn't you say so?'

As if that was all it took to explain why I'd handed her this duster that was likely older than she was.

'So hard-headed, parents,' she giggled as she put pins on the garment to prepare it for darning. 'And so set in their ways.' The other seamstresses shared in the joviality. 'You know the elderly . . . they like what they like,' she smiled, handing me a receipt.

I took it immediately, wondering why I had lied. My mother had been dead for years. But instinctively, I let the seamstresses believe she was alive because it was easier than admitting that I've kept most of her dusters—and they're all I wear when I am at home. The one I'd taken in for mending was the oldest of the collection and had been her favourite. I don't care that the 'old lady' dusters might be 'uncool' or seen as tacky. They're my mother's and that's all that matters. I wear them because they're comfortable and keep her near, and when I'm feeling low, it's like being wrapped in her reassurance.

It has not been easy to navigate the years in my mother's absence, so many questions that I wish I had asked her. And as I struggled to fit into my own skin, I bore in mind that, like her duster, I also wore the legacy she left behind.

She told me to pray and trust in the mercy of God—but like I said, I seem to have unconsciously 'quit' the institutionalized opiate. What I do keep is a faith in the cycle of life . . . and a belief that there will always be a shop for mending.

#

Somewhere today I read that tradition is just 'peer pressure from dead people', but in the same feed, there was also a reminder that ancestors leave you more than just wounds.

So, as I grapple with moments of darkness, I find my way through cloaked in the strength my mother left me. And I will keep being clad in her duster . . . making sure to patch any holes that appear in this shield of comfort she always wore.

RANDOM NOTE

'The moment of absolute certainty never arrives . . .
Act as if everything depended on you . . .
And pray as if everything depends on God.'

*From a card I received from my parents after
my college graduation

When I Grow Up

You won't see it coming, but one day you will wake up and find you are the adult in the room. With no clue how that happened. People you know—*from childhood!*—are suddenly running the world. Imagine that? It's insane! To wit: a vapid, timid seat mate from the fourth grade has become senate president. A few other schoolmates are now unaccomplished but long-*sitting* (I am purposely avoiding the word 'serving') local mayors, and many more are running large conglomerates. What. The actual. F*#&! So, this is why the world is so messed up—some punk kid who used to cheat from you in math is overseeing the national budget. *And you were crap at math!*

Clearly, this happens with every generation, but does every generation feel like this? Does every age group look around at their peers and feel lost? Akin to drunks behind the wheel of a rickety car without a map in a storm? Apparently so. But it's also about hiding it. Pretending you know what you're doing. And growing up in the Philippines, what that means is making the most of your childhood connections. People are always so aware of who is linked to whom and how. An outside observer put it thus: on the islands, it's all about *fellowship* and *followship*. Regardless of social standing. It's about who you know—and who's in charge.

So, So-and-So is Such-and-Such's cousin, who once ate stale rice cakes on the playground and pooped his pants. And that Boy who threw the rock at the Young Girl on the Swing is the neighbour's nephew, who is the son of that yada yada who cheats at mahjong, owns the large corner house, and was banging the driver. These things stick, and these recollections matter because, like it or not, they will define the person till the end. So-and-So may find himself head of the tax bureau, but since he is Such-and-Such's cousin—and remember, he knows you know he once pooped his pants—he can help you tweak your tax report. And the country's new autocrat? Oh yeah, he was always a piece of work—remember when he threw that rock at the Girl on the Swing and she landed in hospital needing stitches? Wasn't that just an excuse to cover up her mother getting a nose job? Who knows for sure? And who cares? These so-called backstories are endless, and their veracity rarely matters. Point is: ultimately, every adult in a grown-up job doing important work is really a ten-year-old who once pooped their pants. And someone will always know their dirty secrets. The biggest of which is the fact that they will always be that frightened child. No matter how many pearls they wear or ties they own. How do I know this? Because many of these grown-ups reveal it themselves—if not in what they do, then in what they say.

You might presume from the above examples that I was in some fancy school for privileged children who went on to reach powerful posts—actually, back then, it was pretty much a provincial institution surrounded by dirt roads and grasslands, far from the urban centre of power. Regardless, no matter where we grow up, we all get to a stage where the decisions we make affect not just ourselves but those around us. And I don't know about you—but I am still waiting to feel *ready* for that.

#

An aside: I once found my mother looking at herself strangely in the mirror. She was not a vain woman, so this struck me as particularly odd. Without turning in my direction—but of course aware of my presence, as all mothers seem to have a sixth sense about their children—she stated: 'I still feel like I am twenty-two . . . and then I catch myself in the mirror and can't believe what looks back at me.'

My mother was never one to be vulnerable, and that was the only time she ever spoke of getting older. Now that I think about it, I don't know why I took that brief moment of her confronting her age as a vulnerability, but as Imelda Marcos, aka the mother of the boy-who-cheated-in-school-and-went-on-to-defraud-his-nation, once said: It isn't truth that's real, but perception.[1] So for most of my life, growing older meant becoming fragile. Which is curious, since—aside from my parents—many in my family have lived beyond eight decades. And they did so strong and hearty and raging with opinions. Far from any image of fragility I can conjure. Now that I am closer to their age than my perception of myself as . . . oh, say, twenty-two, I hope to rage beyond my eighth decade as fabulously as they have.

---

[1] Imelda Marcos, former Philippine First Lady, interviewed in *The Kingmaker*, a film by Lauren Greenleaf, 2019.

I'm Mortal•ity

It has often been said 'the young' feel invincible—know why? Because the concept of dying is so far removed from their realities that they don't think it will ever happen to them—or to anyone they know.

And then someone they know dies. Unbeknownst to them, this will change them forever. Inevitably. Death holds the power to shake you, the survivor. Regardless of age, you are suddenly ever so aware that you are not safe. That you will not be spared the same end. If that doesn't freak you out—then, bully for you. I'm kidding. (No, I'm not.)

Death terrifies me. Scratch that. It isn't actually the idea of dying that scares me but what it's made me aware of—that there is a timer on my life. Tick-tock. The biological clock isn't just one for maternity. Great.

I used to feel that everything lay before me yet to be discovered and experienced—but when you are closer to fifty than twenty-five, you *know* that there is more behind you than ahead. Some people see this as a kick up the bum—a boost pushing them to accomplish their dreams. Others may fall into a malaise about the meaning of life and how little they have left to look forward to. I won't bother to tell you which category I fall under. But I will say this: mortality, it weighs heavy. And the realization that time moves swiftly, that you don't have forever on this wretched plane, is a bittersweet one.

I am still searching for motivational aspartame.

RANDOM NOTE

I really, really wish I could have kept the house I grew up in. But I lost it. In a sense. Long story. Won't go into it. The other night, I was tossing and turning more than usual, and when I finally forced myself up from bed the next morning, I found I had jotted this down on my phone:

The house has become the wound
where the pain lives.

Letting Go

Cleaning out some boxes the other day, I uncovered a trove of embarrassing items. Not least of which were scraps of paper from high school filled with broken dreams. Yes, that overly dramatic description is intentional. That's exactly how fifteen-year-old me might have seen it.

On slightly yellowed but crisp-with-age note paper, among the hurried sketches of palm trees and Smurfs, (yes, Smurfs, now leave it be), I had painstakingly written out my full name with calligraphic flourish, capped with the surname of my intended. Of course, said intended had no idea we were in the throes of a deep love affair and soon to be betrothed. But I had it all mapped out: we would marry by twenty-three and have a handful of children before thirty. He would become a dashing, respected businessman and I would be a well-renowned, contented, stay-at-home writer. As it happens, none of that transpired. The great love was nothing more than a figment of a hormonal teen's over-active imagination. The 'intended' turned out to be a spoiled brat only interested in conquests and his next high (way into adulthood, mind you). And the children ... well, the children that never were ... I try not to think about.

These aren't the only formative dreams I had to bury. By my mid-forties, I realized a lot of what I may have hoped for was not to be. I was getting much older than allowed for any of those fantasies. With my eyesight growing poor from too much audio-visual editing and screen time, it was too late to try and become a pilot. And I certainly was too old to become a pop star. Law school may have been a possibility, but I needed to earn a living.

And so, I stuck to TV news. Yes, it was a steady paycheque, but I also truly enjoyed the adventure, the flexible—albeit long—hours, and living off-the-cuff and by the seat of my pants. It was fun to not have a plan and yet make it so everything worked out effectively. Like unravelling balls of knotted yarn and weaving them into beautiful tapestries, on instinct. I enjoyed the travel and the constant motion. The opportunity to always see the world through a visitor's lens—which meant being hyper-observant down to the minutest of details and not taking things for granted. I also enjoyed not having to talk about *my* thoughts or feelings. As a journalist, I had to listen. Not only to what was said, but more importantly, to what was not. I learned to pay attention to the rhythms of the world. To read the silent energies in a room and feel the pulse of a community. Yes, I know that sounds, again, a little overly dramatic or feebly airy-fairy—but what I mean is, I learned to trust my gut. And that has served me well. Even if in the process I had to let go of the dreams that would not come true. I had to let go of the things we learn in childhood we should want—like a spouse and children of our own. The concepts we are taught to define ourselves by as women. Always in relation to something or someone else. Mothers, wives, daughters, sisters, widows.

Mainly, we were taught to define ourselves by where we come from, and when my parents passed, I had to let go of the holders of my childhood. And when I had to do that, something inside me shifted. I found myself suddenly in the position of having to accept that I was now one of the Grown-Ups. That intangible, untenable fiction we create around ourselves. Adulthood. It still doesn't feel right. I am at midlife—*middle-aged*—and still feel like an orphan child, longing to be taken in and cared for. OMG—did I just admit that out loud? Out loud and in writing. But then again, in this day and age, I can always just put that down to #fakenews—I can keep repeating that what you read was wrong or misunderstood and misrepresented. And if I repeat it enough times, both you and I will likely believe it.

The world has become such a place of nonsense. Where we must let go of even the tiniest speck of truth.

But before that, here is *my* truth: I lost my parents, I lost my sense of self, I lost my direction. I looked around in darkness and lost the will to find my way out to the next adventure. I had to let go of my own grief as well as all the trauma I'd witnessed in my line of work. The lines blurred, and I lost the fire that I once felt in my soul. The desire to see the world wore itself out, and I tired of wearing my shadows like a shield. So, I let them consume me. And I walked around like a zombie unable to breathe. Unable to feel. That's when I had to learn to let go of my fictions. Of the stories I told myself about life that no longer served me. I had to let go of my 'strength' and fall apart.

And here's another thing I learned: when you rebuild yourself after that, it is not from zero. There are stanchions and structural posts that remain despite the internal combustion. There are traces of your truth and remnants of recollections that serve as your bricks and mortar for reconstruction. And when you rebuild, you must let go of the metaphorical childhood 'home' you always returned to for solace. Trusting that your new abode is just what you need—at your new stage—to keep you centred.

Is It Hot in Here?

It's become a bit of a joke among people that I know, both colleagues and friends, that I go nowhere without a *paypay*. (Pronunciation guide: pie-pie.) An *abanico* to some, or simply a hand fan. It is practically tethered to me. An extension of my arm. Particularly, the folding Spanish ones that flick open and shut with a twist of the wrist. They fit nicely in my bag or back pocket. No, I didn't just start using them upon hitting middle-age, and I definitely don't wave them around to look like a self-important matron. It is HOT in the tropics, people! (And that's got nothing to do with *peri*menopause. Ahem.) I mean, seriously, how am I even to know for sure what a hot flash is when to me anything above 22 degrees Celsius is scorching? And I've felt like this for as long as I can remember.

The other day, I was walking outdoors on an errand and people on the streets were wearing jackets. Jackets! It was 35 degrees. I don't understand. There I was sweating in shorts, and everyone else looked like they'd just come out of a very icy cinema or a stereotypically air-conditioned call centre. Either that or they were living in a very different reality from mine. I certainly wanted what they were having!

And this is why I always have a paypay on me. Even when in colder climes or air-conditioned rooms. You never know when what is chilly to someone will still not be cold enough for you. It is much easier to manage one's body thermostat with a fan than inconveniencing others with your need to control the climate.

Having said this, I am just now recalling a work assignment that entailed a twelve-hour, overnight drive to the Philippines' eastern coast right before a typhoon. Of course, we didn't know there was a storm coming—yes, I admit, poor planning. Especially for someone who used to present the weather on the nightly news!

Anyway, it took months to set up this very sensitive shoot with some of the most wanted fugitives in the country and there was no way we could reschedule. No matter the weather. So, off we went, five people with a ton of filming equipment and scant personal belongings, crammed into what was technically a modernized jeep—with glass windows that rolled up and air conditioning. When we got to what we thought was our destination, we were led down a steep incline across a river and up a winding mountain path—and down and up and 'round again for another eight hours. By then, it was raining. I slipped a few times and fell into a muddy stream of running water. It was also a very muggy afternoon. I couldn't tell the raindrops from my sweat. I have never done too well in the heat, but I got used to it, particularly when working. So, I always just got on with whatever task there was at hand until the cameraman had me in shot and complained that I looked too red or soggy. Or—in a word—unwatchable.

(An aside: We were filming once on a beautiful stretch of beach that happened to be home to a brutal group of bandits. Not the outlaws I mention above but rather *another* troop of armed men who were considered terrorists on several international watchlists. As you may have surmised, in my line of work, we met a lot of . . . uhm, colourful characters.

(So, we were at this little-seen, beautiful stretch of beach. I wanted to highlight the place by doing a piece-to-camera— that's when a reporter stands in front of a camera and delivers information looking straight down the lens. To not leave ourselves exposed to danger and 'at risk' for too long, I tried to do it hurriedly and was rather perplexed by the cameraman's refusal to film me. I imagined I looked like an overcooked shrimp drowning in sweat, but I insisted he record nonetheless. He was adamant about not wasting time to film something I would not use in the final report, but I insisted. He insisted I 'trust' him. I told him I wasn't vain and just wanted to show the viewers that we were reporting from the heart of the terrorists' lair. He rolled his eyes and filmed as I'd asked. Of course, ultimately, he was right. We didn't use the shot. My face looked like it had been stung by a thousand bees. By the time we got to the car after filming, I was having trouble breathing and they had to rush me to the Red Cross office to get a prophylactic. Turns out, I was having an allergic reaction to some local shellfish they had fed us for lunch.)

Anyway, where was I? Yes, I digress a lot now too. I struggle to focus. I'm easily distracted. My mind is often in a thousand different places at once—and nowhere. Is that a result of undiagnosed long-Covid or a symptom of perimenopause? Dammit—see? Again, I went off tangent . . .

Ah, yes! Filming the NPA—the New People's Army—the communist rebel forces. For decades, a goal for many journalists covering the Philippines. It was never among mine. I didn't dream of trekking into the mountains and wandering into a storm just to speak on camera to some of the country's most wanted people. Go figure. Also, I did not know how I would do being out in the heat that long. For days on end. But then again, as I said earlier, I did get used to it when working. Ignoring any physical discomfort and malaise. And on that trip, despite feeling like I might spontaneously combust from the heat, I was fine . . . until it was time to sleep.

Crammed into a small room that got absolutely no breeze but where we could at least put up a mosquito net—I could not sleep. Despite how tired I was. My friend and producer at the time quite proudly brought out the latest gadget to hit the market—a portable battery-powered fan that you could hold in your hand. But—and this we learned that very first evening—it's nearly impossible to use such a fan and fall asleep. Because every time her eyes shut and her consciousness slipped into slumber, her hand relaxed and the whizzing battery-powered fan fell on her face! So much for beating the heat.

But I do recall a time when the heat didn't seem to affect me at all. I didn't even break a sweat. And to think, it was the height of summer—in Baghdad!

Basically, I suffered a heat stroke. I was outdoors—in the noon day sun, in the middle of August—waiting for a live interview to begin. I was dressed head-to-toe in black. Lord knows why. (It was slimming? And no matter how dirty it got, it never showed?) Anyway, I learned then that this was a mistake. Heat stroke is real. I got back to the bureau as if in a daze. Moving in slow motion and feeling light-headed. Almost like I had had too much wine. I was losing sensation in my extremities, which I was told was not a good thing. I had also effectively stopped perspiring. Again, not good. I couldn't even *feel* the heat. It was more than 50 degrees Celsius outside and I felt cool as a cucumber. Or so I thought. The medic sent me to my room where I was told to remain until I had hydrated enough to feel human again. The dangers of heat exhaustion—I later found out—were quite profound. And here I thought I just felt a little drugged.

Why am I telling you stories about feeling hot? And again, no, I am not currently suffering from hot flashes. I'm almost certain of that. I think. Wait—speaking of hot flashes: a doctor asked me the other day what my mom might have told me about menopause . . . uhm, DUH. As if! Like anyone my age would speak to their mothers about menopause. Or rather, as if the mother of anyone my age in ostensibly conservative Manila would've spoken to their daughters about such a private matter. As you might imagine, such stoicism and silence resulted in many of us daughters learning to be independent and developing an ability to self-soothe. Of course, I didn't know that's what the latter skill might have been called until recently. And for someone who these days can also feel quite distressed, it's a good thing I have picked this up. *Self-soothe.* Sounds so New Age, hippie-dippie. (Yes, I know, using those phrases totally dates me!) But there you go. I am a resourceful self-soother. This might entail hugging a soft baby blankie and devouring chocolate . . . but it works. And it was most helpful when I was employed in news. You don't get far in that job or stay sane unless you find a way to handle the stresses. One way of coping—at least in the moment—is to ignore it. To carry on as if nothing is awry. To focus on what needs to be done and get on with it. Basically, to push past despite the discomfort. Perhaps by using a metaphorical paypay.

But, having said that, I learned the effects of anxiety stay in your cellular memory, whether you are aware of it or not. And at some point, later, it will bite you in the ass.

Perimenopause, or menopause transition, is when your ovaries gradually begin to make less estrogen. It lasts until menopause, the point when your ovaries stop releasing eggs. In the last 1–2 years of perimenopause, this drop in estrogen speeds up.

—WebMD

Estrogen is a hormone that plays a role in both male and female body functions. In females, it contributes to reproductive and breast health, as well as cognitive health, bone health, and the function of the cardiovascular system.

—Medical News Today

Silence Isn't Golden

Speaking of being bitten in the ass . . . (see preceding essay, and no, this isn't about to take a turn towards kink).

My parents were of a generation known for its silence. Born on the tail end, just before the advent of the Boomers. Raised right after the Second World War ended, they were shaped by scarcity and the need for resilience, 'coming of age' during a period of 'societal change' as the world worked to recover from 'immense hardship'. Or so the online info gods explain. Basically, this means that when things got rough, they said little—if anything at all—and carried on regardless.

My mother's generation wasn't known for speaking to their children about things other than schoolwork, employment, and maybe how to dress and behave. Everything else was shrouded in secrecy. So there was no asking them questions about relationships, heartbreak, or things past. I can't even bring myself to put sex on that list (yes, I shrank the font intentionally, think of it as whispered). Imagine a conversation with them about the nuances of gender roles and identity? Yeah, no.

I can't recall who taught me about menstrual periods—but I certainly didn't learn about it at home. Looking back now, I think I have a vague memory of a biology class in the fifth grade. A very brief and awkward lesson with an awkward teacher going on awkwardly about these clearly awkward things. I was around eight or nine and in a co-educational school, but for this special lesson, the boys and girls in our class were divided and put in separate rooms. That's when we girls were taught about sanitary napkins, periods, getting pregnant, et cetera, the sole focus being how to make the next generation. Who knows what the boys were taught. None of our boy classmates told me. And I honestly can't say if this was better or worse than what children go through today. Is it better now that everything is so readily available to everyone? That perhaps there are no more such awkward lessons?

These days, there is certainly less of an excuse for ignorance but also less of a need for an exercise in creativity. If I were a child now, in this hyper-digital age, I would never make the mistake of thinking that babies can just be ordered from doctors' offices—or that young girls can take a pill and blow up like balloons. That was how a teenage pregnancy was once described to me. And yes, I was naïve enough to believe it. My grandfather was a doctor—no, he wasn't the one who told me the story—and I wondered which of his colleagues gave out balloon pills because he didn't seem to. There was another girl who thought that two people lay on top of each other and blew into each other's mouths—and that's how the balloon baby got in the woman's tummy. I have no idea why we seemed stuck on this idea of balloons!

So, in the fifth grade, we young girls were taught about our bodies as the place where babies come from—but was this also how our boy classmates learned sex ed? That it's all about procreation? (*Can you tell I went to a religious school?*) I suppose they focused on teaching females about the *outcome* because it's the women who have to carry and birth the child. But what did we learn from the segregation of the sexes during these lessons? That women bear the responsibility—and boys can just bugger off?

Holy cow, am I losing the plot? Why am I going down a rabbit hole about sex ed? Maybe because in the decades since those awkward classes, little has changed in terms of the balance between the sexes. And you see it everywhere. Sure, we pay a lot of lip service now to female empowerment and gender equality . . . but is there more than that? Yeah, no. I was once offered a foreign posting if I would agree to be paid 'like a local'. I turned down the job only for it to be offered to a younger man with far less experience for 'expat' pay. How do I know this? The guy himself called me—he knew the job should've been mine and wondered why I turned down such a salary. And what this says about how little we value women's work is the least of it.

What about the awful silence that reverberates every time women are violated by men needing to impose their fragile virility? Despite centuries of 'civilization', such barbarity is not a thing of the past. We still read about it daily in our news feeds. The stories of abuse and assault circulate faster now too thanks to social media, normalizing them in a sense, and making the deafening apathy in response even worse. The impotence of the post shares and likes is laughable. And yes, it pisses me off that that is all most of us do.

I do not just mean the gendered horrors inflicted during wartime, there is a pervading macho perversity in social behaviour as a whole. In many parts of the world, a guy can get multiple women pregnant and it's seen as a sign of his masculinity, while the women are scoffed at for being 'loose' or 'stupid'. Have you been around a family discussion when it's let slip that someone was born out of wedlock or the result of an accidental coupling? Things that our elders may be keeping from general knowledge. But in the end, the truth will out and become public information, especially if it's salacious as heck. What is the reason for not discussing what might be painful or ugly or raw? It was considered more genteel to maintain a dignified silence. More educated and cultured to know what to speak of and what was to be kept private.

But we no longer live in a world that can tolerate silence. And though people might not be listening, everyone is screaming to be heard. Not that I blame them. So many of us have been suppressed for so long. Now, there is social media on which everyone and their neighbour's chihuahua can 'post' about their innermost feelings. Their toilet thoughts—people's most personal ponderings whilst seated on a potty, their hardcore heartaches, their guttural gripes, their most intimate intimations. It is so noisy everywhere I can barely even hear myself think. All this time growing up thinking there was too much silence and longing for explanations—and now I just long for pockets of peace. Where I can hear the wordlessness of my uncertainty and the quiet of my shadows. Where I can be alone with the shape of my soul. I imagine there are new parents who might wish the same—and I feel you. But don't. Don't wish for silence like mine. Be grateful for the hive that is a home full of children. Grateful for the demands on your time and attention. You have been given a gift to experience life as part of something greater—but in no way do I see that as the be all of your—or my—existence. We are more than just extensions of our family units. And I for one am learning to be grateful for my . . .

For my . . .

Hmmm . . .

Be right back. While I figure out a way to end that sentence.

Things to look forward to:

- Sagging skin
- Body aches
- White hair
- Extra girth
- Sluggish metabolism
- Endless exhaustion
- Slow reflexes
- Worsening eyesight
- Memory lapses
- Mood swings
- My God, this list is longer than I expected!

Dental Appointment

Dentists have always terrified me. I think it's rooted (see what I did there?) in a visit I paid one when I was child. She kept asking me questions while working on a cavity. I answered, and the drill slipped and nicked my tongue. There was a lot of blood and a lot of bitter hydrogen peroxide. The relationship went downhill from there. The very thought of a dental appointment was enough to cause me heart palpitations and the older I got, the more anxious I became.

'Relax,' my current dentist constantly reminds me when I go in for a cleaning. Easy for her to say—she wasn't on the receiving end of a drill-slip! Her very organized assistant has me scheduled in for an appointment every six months, and each time I am nervous as all heck. Once, she found a cavity that she said needed filling. 'Your choice,' she told me. Choice? Really, what options did I have? Cavity? No cavity? It was a no-choice-r. Right? I was anxious the entire time, gripping the dental chair like I was on a fairground roller coaster. At the back of my mind, a loop was playing of all the horror stories I'd heard. One guy ended up with holes in his tongue that he could put his finger through, another wound up needing surgery to repair a puncture in his nasal passage. These are not stories for the faint of heart—or for a grown up who was a child whose tongue got drilled.

So again, I have a date with my dental torturer. And though she's never done me wrong, I am dreading the half hour I am meant to see her for a cleaning. Because despite the decades that I have gone to her with no mishaps or 'accidents', plus her constant reassurance, I am still that frightened child who got her tongue drilled. And should something go wrong now, I will have to deal with it on my own. There are no actual grown-ups to fall back on for support, and no do over. Compounding it all, at this age, we no longer feel invincible, and we know that one small cavity can lead to a root canal. That even the smallest of health issues can be a major concern.

So, yes, I don't enjoy going in for a cleaning—because I never know what the dentist will find.

Warning: Intruder!

As women, our bodies seem to turn against us for not doing what we were biologically, genetically, meant to: if you don't have kids, you will pay for it. With myomas, cysts, et cetera, that doctors say women 'who don't bear children' are prone to. Almost like Life saying: 'You wasted your uterus, so this is what you get.' Well, if I was not meant to waste my uterus, why was it never quite the right time to have a child? There was no Prince Charming, no co-parent, not even a momentary breath to consider solo parenting. My parents actually told me once that there was no 'right time' to have a child—but that when you did have one, you'd make it work, no matter what. That was their philosophy. If you waited for the 'right time'—they told me—you could end up waiting forever. Well . . . boom.

But I am not alone. So many people I know who are my age—in fact, most of them—are unmarried and un-dependented. Without dependents. Without children. There isn't even a word for it other than 'childless'. Which—let's be honest—just sounds absolutely abysmal.

Regardless, we all reach a stage when we must start seeing more of our doctors. And when we do, they start finding things like lumps and bumps and grey matter that need to be checked and rechecked. By then, for women, our hormones are totally out of whack (like all the time), and fat cells start clumping together in places they didn't used to until you begin to feel like one big, unbecoming blob of *bleh*.

And when you are this unbecoming blob of bleh, there is nothing you will fear more than getting a message after a medical exam saying the doctor wants to see you ASAP. That's usually never an invitation to a party. I can't begin to tell you how stunned I am by the number of people I knew who passed away before they even got to fifty. Strokes. Heart attacks. Aneurysms. And several heartbreaking suicides. Then there are those stricken with cancer. I have a difficult time even writing the word. Both my parents passed away because of it. So, when a routine post-pandemic mammo resulted in a text from the doctor's office saying 'come see her ASAP', you can bet that my head went to a million different places and none of them good.

Honestly, I have no clue how others do it: deal with the realization that there is something in your body that is not meant to be there and could cause you harm. One day, you are fine, and then in a moment—*snap!*—things change. I panicked. Like a coward. I started worrying about all the things I had not done. Had not completed, had not accomplished. Where would I deposit all the *things* I had left unattended? That next novel, for example. I had it all worked out . . . at least in my head. So, who would put it all down on paper for me?

It was a very long few days before I managed to see the doctor. Time spent half in tears or terrified silence. Looking back at every choice I'd ever made, wondering where I should have been more *this* instead of *that*. Or possibly more *that* instead of *this*. So many sudden questions. Like why oh why do we take our health for granted? The early folks were right when they said youth is wasted on the young. Why are we—at any age—so careless with our priceless existence? I can write this now because after that roller coaster in my head, things were not as bad as I had feared. Thank goodness. But it was definitely a wake-up call.

#

On a tangent: I was a huge fan of Olivia Newton-John. Ever since I first saw her in *Grease* performing alongside my childhood idol, John Travolta. She just had such a light emanating from her. Eight-year-old me was convinced she glowed from within. From then on, I followed her career—yes, I even liked her box-office flops *Two of a Kind* and sat through *Xanadu* several times. (What? The music was fab, not to mention Gene Kelly!)

And then, she publicly had to deal with multiple cancer diagnoses. What a soul. Through all that, Olivia Newton-John created an album of music on which the lead single is called 'Help Me to Heal'. We played it on loop for my mom when she was in hospital. I figured if it helped Olivia, it would help my mom. It didn't quite work out for us as we had hoped.

But Olivia got better. She even visited Manila to perform at the age of sixty-two. I was gobsmacked. Sixty-two! Olivia Newton-John performed an entire concert, dancing and all—barely pausing for breath. My grandfather died at sixty-two. So did my father . . . and my mother not long after him. And here was Olivia, dancing and singing halfway around the world from where she lived, after everything her body had been through. The power of her will struck me.

As I write this, Olivia Newton-John has just passed away. At seventy-three. And it hit me as if I lost a favourite aunt. Her cancer had returned. The illness took her and several others much younger than her almost in the same breath. It was a sobering week.

#

There is no telling when your time is up, but an *intruder* doesn't mean you have to lie back and expect the worst.

#

I am at the beach now with a friend who herself has come out on the other side of cancer. And like Olivia, she has come through a much more refined version of herself. She eats differently, treats her body better, and is more aware of the choices she makes. She is recovered, in remission, and is valuing every moment she now has since her diagnosis. She is looking at the world around her with the freshest of eyes. I am in awe. Of her courage and her eager determination to carry on with joy.

May we not need to have intruders knock on our doors to meet life with such wide-eyed grace.

White Flag

No one told me it would feel like the hair on corn stalks. Dry and unyielding. It always looked so silkily silver and elegant on the imposing matrons I saw in the movies. Made them look so wise and all-knowing. I thought I would be *ancient* before that would happen to me. That I would have to go around the old metaphorical block a few hundred times before showing signs of such . . . wisdom. Well, without warning, they just decided to claim real estate on my scalp. I am just glad they haven't taken over completely. This was not the way I thought I would respond to finding the odd white hair. Frankly, I didn't really wonder how I might respond at all because I never really considered it happening to me. We never do though, do we? Consider something as natural as *ageing* happening to us?

They say you always remember your first, and boy do I! The shock of the dead, colourless strand sticking out from my head—I will never forget it. I panicked. What to do? I had heard the old wives' tales warning against pulling it out. If I did so, it would only breed more white hair. And who would want that? Right? What happened to my earlier mentioned appreciation for the silky locks on 'imposing, elegant matrons'? Well, I thought I was *way* too young to be among that flock. That's what.

My mother's hair was white in her thirties. My father died in his early sixties with a full head of hair and not a single white strand. I had hoped that my hair follicles would take after my father.

But then, a tiny wisp or two of white began to show up in my eyebrows. So small you could barely even get a hold of them to pluck. I figured I could leave them alone. Just as I did when the single strand of white in my head turned into two—I left them alone. But then two strands became four, and four, sixteen. You get the idea. Now, I occasionally swing my hair and see the colour of hay. *Hay!* I must admit, it is hard not to succumb to the temptation of pulling them out, but what do you do when sixteen becomes thirty-two? And that progresses to sixty-eight? Sixty-eight strands of white? I swear if I pull any more out, I will look half bald.

A professional hair maven suggested to me that dyeing hair gold would hide the silver. I never thought I could get away with being blond so I kept my hair as it was, trusting I would let myself age gracefully. LOL.

The other day, standing in my youthful summer dress, wearing sneakers and holding my hair back with sunglasses, my nearly eighty-year-old aunt suddenly started to 'weed' my head. She literally yanked out a strand of hair. 'White!' she said with glee. Worse, she then went on to exclaim, 'So many!' Right before attempting to dive back in. I was horrified. Up until then, I had fooled myself into believing there were maybe one or two 'visitors' but definitely not enough to qualify as 'many'!

Pop went my bubble of denial. Ah, family, you can always count on them to bring you crashing back to Earth!

But then again, there is also the other end of the spectrum. It does seem like more people—I can name at least two ;)—are choosing to let their hair be as natural as can be. It suits them and they somehow look younger. Go figure. Maybe because they aren't stressed about trying to seem anything other than what they are. The ease with which they flow into getting older shows in a youthful glow that beams off their faces. That could be the trick. Non-resistance and acceptance. So, if it's time for hay, then hay it is. Even people of younger generations are *choosing* to shock in white. The guy serving coffee the other morning looked about twelve years old and had a long ponytail whose tip was dyed a smoky ash-white. Apparently, it's been a trend for nearly a decade, with pop stars and actors leading the way. Shows you how clued in I've been lately.

Sigh.

But . . . I'm no pop star or Hollywood influencer. No Helen Mirren or Emma Thompson, both of whom are so at ease in their skin. I mean, I thought I had that same unapologetic self-confidence. A nonchalance about how I appeared. I guess I was wrong. Because here I am struggling with a few greys and being older. Unable to even remember my real age because I stopped counting at forty. Okay, I lie, I stopped counting at thirty-five. I feel like if I know the real number and envision it, it would signify a countdown, and the last thing I want to be reminded of is an expiry date.

Yes, there I've said it—I am terrified. I am afraid to even admit that to myself. So instead, I tell myself all sorts of fictions to be able to act like I am still the girl I feel like inside. If age is just a number, I don't understand why I am increasingly unable to lose weight no matter the diet or why my back aches even before I get out of bed. Speaking of bed, is anyone else afraid to lie down at the night? Worried of the pain that being supine will elicit? Any other *young-ish* person feel like this?

I don't know what it is I am saying any more—I just know that seeing the whites on my head can be upsetting. I guess I am not as cool about it as I would have liked to be—or as comfortable in my skin as I thought. That strand of hay taunts me like a dagger. What I wouldn't give to be invincible to the jab.

If like me, you are ducking a duel, I will leave you with that tip from a pro—for those who have the desire and the means, dye your hair blond so any whites disappear into a bale of gold. As for me, I have resisted the conversion to a facsimile of Marilyn Monroe but have taken on the copper tones of a glorious sunset. Perhaps when I wake tomorrow, I will care less about hiding any strands of *hay* and will have learned how to ease gracefully into my stage of imposing, elegant wisdom.

DOES IT REALLY MATTER?

A Million Miles from Paradise

There are days you just can't get out bed. Yes, this is another one of those. I feel disembodied and unfamiliar. Like a transparent corpse that doesn't occupy space or time. I had been feeling like this for a while before someone suggested it might be my hormones. *Hormones?* I wondered. WTF? I was long done with puberty, what would hormones have to do with anything? Was it a problem with my thyroid? That sort of thing is genetic, isn't it? Wouldn't that also explain weight gain and mood swings? And energy fluctuations and the lack of concentration? I went to the doctors I was advised to go to—and no one could or would explain my malaise. My blood pressure was fine. My heart was okay. My thyroid functioned as it should.

Again, the 'peri' word was being bandied about. I didn't really know anything about it. My mother's generation seemed to go from childbearing years to *non*-childbearing years with ostensibly nothing in between. Now there was this whole *peri* stage. And it had online support groups popping up everywhere. Gosh, was it really something that I should be worrying about? If so, why hadn't anyone warned us about this before? I didn't want to do any research for fear of what I would find.

And then I went to see a gynaecologist. A gamut of blood tests was done on top of an ultrasound. Next thing I knew I was being prescribed a transdermal gel and some sort of capsule I had to ingest at the same time. I thought I understood why. To balance my hormones in some way? I had been seeing this doctor for years and she assumed I knew what was going on, while I made the same presumption about her and didn't ask many questions. Turns out, I had been put on HRT—hormone replacement therapy. I didn't realize what exactly it was or how long I was meant to be on it. I just did as advised. Without even checking a list of pros and cons. So much for applying my journalistic skills to my own life! Once I started on the regimen, I think I began to feel better. I just no longer felt as out of whack. Was the HRT inconvenient to administer? Indeed. But I carried on regardless, without a clue as to how controversial the whole thing was.

Eventually, posts about HRT began popping up on my social media feed. People I knew started whispering about it and asking each other questions. There were all sorts of articles appearing online with lots of negative things to say on the subject—among them, that it could increase the risk of heart problems or breast cancer. Well, dang. I hadn't realized that. I should have been paying more attention. Many women were saying that they'd never heard about HRT but when they looked into it, they decided against it, worried about the risks of taking 'fake' hormones. But others said there were greater risks to leaving any hormonal imbalance *un*-addressed. Bone disease, cognitive decline, and also, cancer. Who to believe? Every woman's experience was unique, and doctors' recommendations seemed to vary. 'Fake', not fake. Bio-identical, synthesized. Take in moderation, go for broke. So many questions being posed, including—were these the same hormones taken by people undergoing gender reassignment?

I will not even presume to give you answers. As I have mentioned, there are support groups, medical papers, and doctors specializing in helping women through peri. All just a click away. And I know we won't all agree despite the information.

The last few days, trending on news feeds along with the usual dystopian headlines was a raging debate over whether the female 'midlife condition' is being over-medicalized. There were those who argued that something *natural* was being turned into an ailment or health problem in need of treatment, as if it were a disease or an infection. They stressed that for centuries, women have 'survived' their age-related, midlife biological transition just fine, so why should it now be any different? But others pointed out that the hormonal imbalance that occurs after a woman's childbearing phase can cause such debilitation that they've had to ask to be let off work or resign because they are struggling both physically and mentally, making them less 'productive' in general. This is itself a controversial concept, as if being in this biological stage of life were a disability.

As I write this, rules have been put in place in Britain by an Equality Commission, allowing women to sue employers for 'disability discrimination' if they're not allowed 'reasonable adjustments' to their work life due to peri/meno symptoms, such as lack of sleep or brain fog. These adjustments include starting work later in the day or indeed staying home to work from there. Are they basically implying that women are or might be less productive because they're no longer *re*-productive? Going by the news articles, some women find this development preposterous, feeling like they run the risk of being seen as 'unhinged wimps' in need of 'a fan and a lie-down'. Women, they say, have been fighting for equality for so long and now the female body itself has become the vehicle for differential treatment? But isn't that just the way it is? Women are not built like men and *should* be treated differently. I am not saying we should be taking sick days or asking for 'special treatment' when we get a migraine, but if we—male or female—are not feeling one hundred per cent, for whatever reason, whyever should we not take a break? What I take issue with is being treated as *less* than or as if we are weaker should we do so. All the strongest people I have met, through emotional and physical trauma, have been women. And I'm not even talking about childbirth. But this is not a matter of which gender is 'better'. Each has its distinctions coupled with personal, individual traits. Ultimately, people are people—and gender is part of their identity, not its entirety.

Speaking of gender, I can't begin to tell you how many male doctors—none of them gynaecologists—advised me to do myself 'a favour' and have a hysterectomy. 'Why not?' one of them said, 'you haven't used it, just take it out.' As if the uterus were like tonsils or an appendix, the removal of which has little impact on the body's performance. They made clear that keeping reproductive parts after they've ceased to serve a purpose could only lead to health issues down the line. But what these men don't realize is how much of our identities might be attached to these organs, whether functional or not. Frankly, I didn't realize that either. Not until the possibility of being without them was before me. Yes, I know that my womanhood isn't down to these 'parts', but dare I say, sometimes it is the little bits inside that reaffirm it. I am speaking only for myself, of course. I mean, how would these men feel if we casually said let's just take your balls to protect you from cancer in the future?

And though it might seem like it, I am not a million miles from my initial intention. Which was to tell you about my ignorance on the matter of HRT, and I know I am not alone in this. What I've now also realized is that *how* we understand our bodies, and our feelings with respect to it, can affect our sense of identity. Taking bio-identical hormones like oestrogen and progesterone is meant to help with the discomforts of transitioning from our reproductive years to our no-longer-reproductive years. A biological shift that can leave women feeling *un*-like themselves. But that is not the case. Through the ups and downs, the cracks and the greys, we always are who we are, and we should do what we can to dispel our own ignorance. Go research to find information that may be missing, speak to multiple (!) doctors, and ask any knowledgeable friends. Remember, though, that as well-intentioned as they might be, each one can only speak from their own understanding.

So when choosing what course to take with our bodies may seem like a gamble, it is up to us to learn to bet on ourselves.

Haemorrhoids

Let's begin with the spelling. Yes, I know that is not the most striking thing about the heading for this chapter—but I also know that those of you who read 'American' will wonder why there seems to be an extraneous letter there. Well, I did my master's in London and lived in the city for the better part of a decade, and that's one of the foibles or habits , if you will, that has stuck with me. No, not the actual medical condition specified in the chapter heading but the spelling. British spelling, to be precise. (Doing a master's in literature, can you imagine the countless essays I had to write using the aforementioned orthography? It stays with you, believe me.)

Years after I left the UK, my spelling—for the most part— has remained anchored on its shores. It somehow feels more— considered. Oh gosh, how much of an Anglophile does this make me sound? I am not, I promise. *Ahem.*

So anyway, how does spelling affect one's understanding of the world? I suppose it shouldn't—a word is just a word after all, isn't it? But here's the thing: word choices, spelling choices—the presence or absence of a single letter—can change the inference or connotation of a word. The subtexts and the assumptions around it. Spelling says so much more about the writer than one might imagine. It reflects an intentionality. And speaks to the writer's thoughtfulness. I would trust a person who takes the time to get it *just so* over one who would use a shortcut. Who would write *text* instead of *txt*. Or full phrases over *hru* and *btw*. Is this a consequence of getting older? Maybe. Of course,

I am aware that meaning is meaning no matter how it gets across, and brevity doesn't necessarily affect clarity—but, I mean, WTF?

Yes, I know, language evolves, as I am constantly reminded merely by seeing—through no choice of my own—how the TikTok generation communicates. Seriously, I have no clue what these post-Gen-Z people are writing/saying most of the time. But the older I get, the less I actually care. Is that bad? Does it make me feel any less relevant and connected to reality? Of course it does! But it also doesn't worry me too much. Because not being up to date with expressions or turns of phrase doesn't make me feel any less alive. Them young'uns have their way of digesting experiences and their existence in the world, just as every generation before them has its own shorthand. (Am I right or amirite?)

I mean, hurrah for those who traverse the boundaries of age—but I am grateful to still be writing in sentences. To spell without vowels missing. Indeed, to be counted among those who might write with seemingly superfluous 'extra' letters. Or occasionally, what may appear to some as a few *extra* words. For me, they create a rhythm to move you distinctly through the text.

Ultimately, this is not about British spelling over American— but language and how we use it. It's a reflection of how we approach the world. Fewer students these days, for example, take handwritten notes in class, preferring instead to record lectures on their devices or type away on their laptops. There are studies that show this corresponds with less retention and processing of information. Some reports go as far as saying it also hampers the development of critical thinking. But handwriting *forces* you to engage. In a classroom setting, you have to focus on what's being said then process that information to put it down on the page. Having to write it by hand slows down your pace almost in meditation. You have to be present and deliberate. And if you engage with material like that, you can't help but retain it. One study by the National Center for Biotechnology Information, a US government agency, also found that those who write things down by hand are in a more 'positive' mood during the learning experience. Perhaps because the mind can't be wandering around to matters that might otherwise cause concern or induce negative thoughts. You can't worry about anything else when you are concentrating on the task at hand, literally. And there's a lot to be said about being more deliberate.

When I was in the field newsgathering, I always had a notebook with me. Not only to take down immutable data but also to gather my thoughts. If something stood out, I wrote it down. If someone said something in a way that revealed more about them than the camera might detect, I wrote it down. The mood at a scene, my impressions, how people moved or interacted, if anything was striking or remarkable, if there were distinctive smells or sounds, whatever it was that either called attention or shied away from it, I wrote it down. But when it came time for scripting the news report, I barely looked at my notebook. Only a glance or two to make sure I got the immutable data right. Everything else I tried to communicate in my pieces was *imbibed* when I wrote things down while in the field. As such, every story was distinct. Every story had a feel. I took them all in discretely. And as they were each their own, that hopefully reflected in the final output.

What am I trying to say? That writing things down by hand helped me be more intentional. It helped me process information faster and be more discerning when moving through the world. I could focus, I paid attention, I was engaged. It was the same as taking the time to write down extra letters in British words.

But then, there comes a time when the world as you know it is tilted off its axis. Because something shifts that you don't expect to. At work, in relationships, or—knock on wood— perhaps your health. Reminding you that you don't have control over everything, no matter how considered and measured you might be. And that instability can keep you up at night, jousting powerlessly with your fears. So, I take a pen to defend against the darkness, seeking certainty in the fluidity of language. Words,

words,

words

help me sort through what to let go of . . .

and give me strength to then set it free on the page.

What I mean is, despite the transitional nature of our existence, there are things in life that can never be denied. There is pain, there is loss . . . and there is love. And while in their throes, words—like haemorrhoids, regardless of spelling—can help ground who we are.

Holy Wood

Working from home can at times make one feel like a caged animal. I am not saying always . . . but, indeed, frequently. Thing is, despite the psychological risks of being cooped up within four walls and the potential of descending into catatonia, I stay indoors because it is more economical. Or so I thought until I realized that thanks to the pandemic, I could still order everything in. Food, coffee, desserts, medicine, clothing, even toilet paper. I need never leave the flat. Which means the place has turned into what one might expect of a teenager's dorm room. Not just my bedroom, but the entire apartment. I have two laptops set up on stands and going at once, papers and books are strewn everywhere, and all sorts of writing implements are competing for space with dust particles on every available surface. I would describe it to you more but suffice it to say I am quite put off by the deterioration of my once orderly cocoon. Albeit solely for personal use, the unkempt space has eaten away at my inner peace instead of fostering it. Some mornings, I wake up and immediately feel hassled by the chaos. Even before I get out of bed and see it.

To try and get myself in the right headspace for work—i.e., writing—I have now taken to starting the day with t'ai chi or qigong. The slow, deliberate movements of the traditional Chinese practices are a wonderful way to calm any anxious or stress-filled energies. It's basically meditation with movement. Perfect for anyone who doesn't like to sit still. But since writing entails a lot of sitting, this is a great way to move the body and get the blood flowing. I can't tell you how surprised I was to discover that there are 'injuries' related to being seated. Having spent so much time as a journalist out in the field and *not* behind a desk, I didn't know there could be shooting pain up the arms because they're bent for so long when typing on a keyboard. There are dull, throbbing aches related to using a mouse, and excruciating discomforts that result from being hunched over a laptop for extended periods of time. I got the ergonomic chair and the jelly-cushioned seat just to make the long-term sitting more bearable. Problem was, I got so comfortable in the position, I rarely stood up. And that caused my hips to tighten. Who knew that could happen?! The sensation can be agonizing, often making sleep impossible. (Adding yet another reason to an already lengthy list.) And I haven't even mentioned the neck yet. Imagine what it's like to have your eyesight worsening, which then leads you to stretch your neck forward so you can better read the screen. The whole endeavour results in terrible posture. And here I thought it was working the field that would leave me somewhat physically compromised. (Actually, it did. My neck and back have yet to recover from multiple car accidents. The whiplash coupled with the writing posture—and I am usually a ball of pain.)

So, there's the bedlam in my space, the pain of the physical writing exercise, and the anxiety of not being able to fill the page. Left alone in this purgatory, I am sometimes driven to tears. Which is what prompted this essay.

It was early afternoon. I had just consumed the salad I had delivered for lunch and was pondering whether I should put in an order for a bubble milk tea. There were other matters I had to attend to while the blank page stared at me, waiting. Although I do consultation work and contribute professionally to other projects, I had set this time aside to do some writing. I had set aside the entire week. It was Friday, and the week hadn't quite gone as hoped. Just short of bursting into tears (again), I realized it was time to bring out the big guns. On top of a corner table by the sofa, I have what look like twigs in a small container. They're each about three inches long and have their ends burned black. Next to them rests a lighter. I take the least burned stick and put it to the flame—waiting until it catches. The smoke is what I'm after. It climbs to the ceiling like a gossamer thread and the smell of it as comforting as incense. I take a deep breath, allowing my heart to ease as the scent of the Palo Santo hugs me from within. The fragile peace it offers lasts for a fraction of a second. I open my eyes and am thrust back into the chaos of my life.

WTF am I doing? I can't keep staring at this mayhem. My words do nothing more than add to the anarchy. In need of a lifeline, I look for the smoke of the Holy Wood, but it's billowed itself into oblivion.

The room I am in is now drenched in a rusted copper as the sun begins to set outside. My back is aching and my eyes are getting weary, so might you excuse me? I think I need to get up off my bum and take a walk. The sun is setting, and I am in need of its fading light to balm my soul.

aka

Truly, how much worse can this get?

One Step at a Time

It may come as no surprise that I am a huge fan of bright, boppy, pop music. I love expansive, upbeat tempos peppered with lively kitsch and glitter. So, seventies disco with its colourful lights, mirror balls, and sequins are a huge hit with me. As is this one particular late-nineties-early-noughties sensation that embodied the very same spirit.

This is just a long way to tell you I am a massive fan of the British pop group Steps. If you've never heard of them—and it was only when I left the UK that I realized they might not be as widely known as I thought—do search for them online. You will not be disappointed. (Or maybe I'm just projecting?)

But seriously, such gloriously joyful music. I feel light just thinking about it. And I dare you to *not* smile when you watch a Steps video. They even turned the Bee Gees original 'Tragedy' into an undeniably happy dance tune. *Tragedy*!

When I was living in London, I once met up with some colleagues in a pub right after a massive CD sale in the four-floor music store around the corner from the office. (Wow, everything in that sentence dates this story!) Anyway, I came out of the sale with only two albums. I believe one may have been a compilation of Shirley Bassey hits and the other was a limited edition of *Steptacular*. (Don't you just love that title? Tee-hee.) As I took my seat at the pub, I put the bag with the compact discs behind me. Not because I was embarrassed by my purchase, there was just no other place to keep it out of view and from being nicked. Well, a lot of good that did—a colleague spotted the bag and asked to see what I had inside.

'You have got to be joking!' he suddenly exclaimed.

A response I wasn't expecting. Was he surprised by the Shirley Bassey or the combination of the two CDs? Perhaps he was wowed by my eclectic taste in music? Nope. It was neither of those options.

'Who the hell listens to Steps?!' he was horrified.

I felt judged. But in truth, it didn't matter. I have always stood firm on my choices and my preferences. So I am not ashamed to be a Steps fan. Ahem.

I ended up working with this colleague even after I left our then employer. We resigned not long after each other and joined the same new company, moving across the globe to open a branch office together in Asia. We spent the next decade working side by side . . . and he never got over the fact that I listened to Steps. It coloured our working relationship forever. And I think he always took me just that little less seriously. But I mean, come on, just because I was a news correspondent didn't mean I had to be grave and dour. It was *especially* as a journalist that I had to hold on to anything that could spark joy. Right?

This was not meant to be an ode to *Steptacular*, Steps, or their multi-platinum career. Which by the way saw a resurgence in 2011, when they reunited after disbanding a decade earlier. The five members—Claire, Lisa, H, Faye, and Lee—went on to keep making music together while simultaneously maintaining solo careers, seeing the group through to their twenty-fifth anniversary since forming. Okay. Now this sounds like an ode to Steps!

But I have a point. Hang with me. I started writing this after getting an online notification that one of the group members was going live on a social media platform. (Okay, so maybe I do keep track of their solo endeavours.) And considering I was in a different time zone, I thought it a stroke of luck that I could join and watch the session as it happened. Indeed, two decades on and Steps still brings me joy.

. . .

So . . .

Uhm . . .

Right . . .

Right.

Turns out, that 'live' wasn't quite what I was expecting. Was this the algorithm's fault? Did something about my scrolling and social media use make the platform think this content was right for my profile? Was my device *eavesdropping* on my conversations? Was it reading my mind? Had technology gone further than publicly acknowledged? Or could it really just be that I got a notification about this special live online session because I am one of Faye Tozer's nearly 200,000 followers? But I am following over 900 accounts (apparently)—so why out of all of them did I get *this* particular notification and not any others?! Was I offended? Uhm, no. Not really. Just surprised that this was now the content that popped up on my feed.

Dear readers, just as announced on that platform, it was indeed step-tacular Steps member Faye . . . live, in online conversation with an older woman I didn't recognize. They were speaking about—wait for it—perimenopause. The eternally vibrant Faye Tozer. *From Steps!* Talking about perimenopause— live, online. Like WHAT!? Our generation could barely get our mothers to speak about such intimate matters and now our pop stars were open to having these discussions in public? Let me tell you, this was not what I was expecting when I clicked on that live session on social media.

Turns out, the other woman gave up her day job a few years prior to devote her time to running a menopause support group. A support group! As if it were an ailment that needed treatment. Oh gosh, was it an ailment that needed treatment? That has opened a floodgate of questions.

Their chat was UK-centred, so I rang up my long-time pals in London to speak to them about the issues raised. We'd seen each other through many *transitional* phases—unemployment, broken hearts, failed diets—so who better to dissect these matters with? Well, as they told me, it seems there's been a trend among British Gen X celebrities—whom we used to watch on morning television or listen to on the radio—now writing books on the physiological changes they're experiencing. They're appearing on shows and on stage to share about hormonal fluctuations, metabolic slowdowns, et cetera, seeing it as a service to other women. They aim to dispel ignorance by promoting greater understanding of a reality that impacts half of the world's population. There are medical professionals now becoming experts in this particular stage of life, as well as health centres dedicated to women searching for information and guidance. These sources reassure that women of a certain age are not 'going crazy' and there are likely hormonal reasons for feeling overwhelmed, depressed, or anxious. There are statistics to back this up too. Unsurprisingly, more than 40 per cent of women don't really understand what they are going through. But more and more seem to be talking about peri or meno. Yes, this is what I am seeing people call it, like they're old pals come 'round for tea, Peri and Meno. There are discussions about the old pals becoming too medicalized with expert opinions weighing in on whether to address the hormonal imbalance or just the symptoms. There are even TED talks on the subject. As much as women of a certain age are being reassured and told that these physiological changes don't have to take over their lives, with everything I'm reading and seeing, it appears a more major event than I realized.

And men, don't think you are spared. Have you heard of andropause? You, too, go through a period of hormonal adjustment. Of course, it pales compared to what the female body goes through, but it is nonetheless a reality. As they get older, the males of the species see a decline in testosterone levels, but it happens over a longer stretch of time and doesn't cause as much discomfort. Resulting physiological changes include slower metabolism, weight gain, a drop in bone density, hot flashes or *flushes*, decreased energy, loss of concentration, and depression. But again, medical websites highlight that this in no way compares with what women undergo. This is not meant to be a diatribe on the differences between the genders but an illustration that there are physical markers signifying an inevitable transition for both men and women.

For want of my mother or anyone older who I can ask, my similarly aged friends maintain that it is just another stage of life and should not be treated as if something is over . . .

But when your body is no longer what it *was*—what then?

Most of the conversations around it say that the important thing is having support, a partner who is there for you, friends, a medical expert. Which is really what community is about. So there must be a reason for all these support groups online. I must tell you, I spent a long time on this group call, speaking about the subject with my similarly aged friends in London—which is more than I imagine my mother doing with her friends. There are books entitled *Me and My Menopausal Vagina* and articles called 'Menopause is going Mainstream' and 'Women Have Been Misled About Menopause', as if it were a trend that may come and go or a state secret that was kept from general female-dom. Ultimately, like with everything else that is out there and now available for greater perusal, people have to make their own decisions. And what is best for each one will come down to individual choice on what's appropriate for them.

It's helpful, I suppose, that a wider community of celebrities is now happily sharing their two cents' worth, but we shouldn't be taking their advice because they have platinum albums and hit TV Shows. Let's certainly appreciate that they are contributing to the library of experiences that people can take into consideration when making their own choices.

Everyone will go through this age-related life change . . . and as evidenced by Faye, we should all just take it one *Step* at a time!

DO I MAKE A DIFFERENCE?

Marching into Consequence

As I write this, it's almost the third month of the year, and you must know what that means. Women everywhere are enjoined to celebrate their significance—to of course match up to the dearth of appreciation for the XY-chromosomed creatures of the species. #sarcasm

After much historical struggle, a day was first set aside in Europe in 1911 to mark the achievements of women. The United Nations officially named an International Women's Day sixty-four years later. In 1987, the US government turned that day into a month and of course the rest of the world followed suit.

Now, in the run-up to March—Women's (History) Month—you can look around and there will be posters, articles, special episodes or editions of shows, magazines, and whatnot featuring 'women of substance'. As much as I can appreciate highlighting people for their achievements, calling attention to their gender in relation to it makes it seem as if the others in that category are insubstantial. No? Are women in general so frivolous that those who aren't seen as such must be noted for their consequence? Tell that to an uncelebrated single mother working three jobs to feed a family. Or a non-famous widow trying to keep going while grappling with heart-rending grief. And what about the many sons who struggle to stay sane in the aftermath of calamity so they can sustain their community? Well, men are generally expected to make a difference or seen as important *just because,* so there is rarely the need to focus on 'men who matter' or men of substance. This only speaks to the massive imbalance between the genders in our cultural realities—for all the 'progress' made, men still dominate and women have to fight for space.

But celebrity or maleness shouldn't be the construct by which to judge what or who matters. Just because someone isn't 'famous' or renowned doesn't mean what they do or who they are is of no significance. Why is the world so obsessed with celebrity? It sets people apart and drives a pursuit of praise. Is that what makes someone feel like they matter?

If I learned anything working as a journalist, it's that all people—each and every person—are consequential. Whether the general public acknowledges that or not. The world is inherently relational and no one lives in a vacuum. Even the most seemingly isolated and detached affect their surroundings. And those who build walls are only deluding themselves.

Who among us hasn't wondered if they matter? Or if they make a difference? Isn't this one of humanity's biggest existential questions? How do you measure that? What will satisfy as an answer? International recognition? A Nobel prize? Platinum records? A Wikipedia page? Does any of that matter? Is that what motivates you? Why do you do what you do? And when will it feel like enough?

Next time I ask myself any of those questions, I am almost certain my own answers will change. Why? Because we change. And what we want or what we think we want evolves too. As much as I might sometimes still feel twenty-two, I know that I am not after the same things I wanted at that age. Well, not entirely. These days I just long to get enough sleep. Maybe to walk in the park at dusk or sit somewhere with a view enjoying a coffee and the page. Does that make me insubstantial? Does it mean I don't matter? Should I be concerned?

And what of the many people who can't faff about pondering these silly existential questions? Is a less examined life a less 'substantial' one? What an inane idea. (With apologies to Socrates.) Tell that to the millions struggling to actually survive while in the crosshairs of the world's dysfunction. War, injustice, poverty, abuse. With all that considered, what then is substantial? Who is of consequence or significant? And if I sit on my ass doing eff-all to help improve someone else's lot in life—do I even matter?

Is the point of it all to live a life of consequence . . . if not, you're inconsequential?

RANDOM NOTE

I just found an essay I wrote in high school and was struck by the teacher's note on it:

'Almost but not quite.'

I think that thought has haunted me ever since.

Betrayed

'Did you know?'

The indignation was clear in her voice when my friend asked us that question on a transcontinental group call.

'And if you did, why didn't you tell me?'

She then turned her attention to the offender. 'I was so good to you . . . I didn't sleep around . . . I didn't do drugs . . . so, why? Why . . . why would you turn on me?!'

She was talking to her body about its age-related changes. As she fervidly put it, she felt—

'—betrayed! It wreaks havoc with your life and no one warned me!'

She had just turned fifty. She felt unattractive, unhinged, and put upon. Not a combination that made her want to be in company. All of us on the call had our cameras off.

'Are you mad?' she said, still indignant. 'I don't want anyone to see me like this. I'm so bloated I feel as big as a whale! I don't recognize myself.'

For a moment, she wondered if she might have fallen miraculously pregnant. It would've explained missing a few months' periods.

'I thought I was chosen by God,' she jested, 'but God, was I wrong.'

She seemed at once joking and deadly serious. She was understandably emotional and felt like she was reaching the end of her proverbial rope.

'They say that it doesn't take over your life . . .' she shared, 'yeah right! What's there to take over when life as you knew it *is* over?!'

Her tendency towards the dramatic has been a long-standing trait that cannot be blamed on recent age-related physiological changes.

'No one gets it,' she concluded. 'It's like I've been betrayed by my best friend—and I am grieving the loss of all else that might have been.'

She was of course talking about the body's dreaded 'pause'. Her symptoms had been so bad they affected her quality of life, but she was refusing to look into treatment. 'I don't need it. I don't want to add hormones to this mess just to deal with *natural* conditions.'

Speaking on a podcast called *It Can't Just Be Me*, popular British presenter Kate Thornton compared her experience of peri to being burgled, as if one's home was repeatedly broken into and their sanity taken piece by piece. 'And then, [you're] expected to perform at the top of your game in every role in your life—be it as a friend, a partner, a mother, a professional— it's too much to ask of women … and it almost broke me.'

She went on to say it turned her into 'chaos on legs', and she was espousing hormone replacement therapy because it helped her feel like herself again.

'It can sometimes feel like being lost in a storm on our own—' another friend on our group call shared. 'But what we need isn't hormones, it's *human* support overall.'

She's not the only one of that opinion. Coping medically *unaided* with the mental anguish, the emotional heaviness, and the physical discomfort that accompanies this life change has long been portrayed as a sign of strength. And that was echoed in this transcontinental conversation. We had all been taught that strong women pull up their boots and carry on regardless.

'It is like being sent off to battle totally unprepared . . .'

'Yeah . . . and much of the conflict is with ourselves—'

'—and everything around us!'

The laughter was tinged with a hint of exasperation. As invincible as we might have once thought ourselves, when the body begins to show signs of . . . not being as it was, mortality hits you in the face.

'I was never terrified of dying . . .' one of my friends started. 'But the minute I turned fifty, there it was. Like having a rug pulled out from under you.'

But she immediately qualified that statement, saying that as she saw it, there were two sides to this 'turning fifty'. Becoming a so-called Golden Girl also made her feel more sure of herself than ever. 'Gave me license to *not give a toss* about what anyone says or thinks . . .' she giggled, shocked at the indelicacy of her admission. She had always been so polite and well-spoken. 'Ah, well,' she sighed, 'I know who I am, and that's that.'

No apologies, no regrets.

'What is the point of regretting anything?' she posited. 'So many of our generation are stigmatized for being single and childless, but why brood? There are other things to be grateful for. So, just get on with it. You just get on with it.'

She proceeded to list a number of things that could be considered positives, including the ability to travel freely. Responsible only for yourself.

'People just got used to a *binary* attitude about things,' she stated, 'but this is not a binary world. Things are not only black or white.'

In other words, you may be single and sans offspring, but that doesn't mean you have *failed*.

My friend. Definitely someone to be thankful for.

'It is regret that is making people sick,' she went on. 'I know someone who works in a home for seniors. And what he saw was that it was those with regrets that were unhappiest. I tell you, treat people well and don't spend your life wishing for something you don't have. All life is valid. And all is good.'

At this point, I would have happily sat back on a pillow and burned some incense. Eager to just take in more of her learnings. I have known the women on this call for decades, and we've all seen each other through a myriad of changes.

'People who think nothing changes are lying to themselves, and age may just be a number—'

'—but it might as well be 666!'

More laughter, tinged with just a touch of nostalgia.

'Do you wonder if you've achieved what you set out to?' I asked.

'What for? Just enjoy the journey. Carry on—because what other choice is there? And then you settle into the age you're in.'

We spoke for hours and it was re-energizing. Helped me feel more appreciative and more aware of where I was at. I was also more confident about being free of other people's expectations and worries. Excited to get back out there after keeping life, for a time, at arm's distance.

So much has passed in the years I've felt unable to engage. The people who have defined my generation are now elderly, but they all seem to be raging towards seniority with fire.

'At what age are we supposed to change our underwear?'

I was surprised by the unexpected sudden question on the call.

'High leg, thongs, they no longer work for me,' the questioner went on, 'but OMG, I really don't want to wear granny panties!'

'Yes, you do. Trust me, you do.'

The loud cackling was warm and familiar. And it felt as if we were back in a pub on an easy weekend shooting the breeze.

'You know in France, the sixties are now the golden decade,' the sage among us said. 'And those in their seventies are still considered youthful.'

'Yeah right,' the less optimistic one ventured. 'Tell that to my dry, dry skin.'

'I love my skin now,' the sage again. 'It's so soft and—'

'—crepe-y?'

'I was going to say velvety . . .'

And the conversation took another jovial turn. We went on like this for a few more cycles. Here's what I picked up that I now want to share:

Don't spend your life waiting for something to 'happen'— you don't want to be a spectator to your own reality. You don't want to get older having just sat back watching other people's lives unfold, as if waiting for your own to catch up.

'I wish I knew sooner how quickly everything goes . . .'

The nostalgia hung heavy over all of us.

This was a conversation none of us would have been able to have with our mothers, thank goodness for friends who are generous with their vulnerabilities.

And with everything said, we reached no categorical conclusion on whether these age-related physiological changes are something you 'treat' or ride out. Are you meant to go with the flow, as it were, or get 'diagnosed' and prescribed medication so that you can be 'better'? Is that what it's about? Being better? At what? Being older? How is one medicated for that? Is the roller coaster of emotions something that needs to be 'fixed' and treated? And if so, what then is *real*? What is our own? If everything needs to be balanced and sorted as if it were out of whack?

I tried to read some of the material that is now out there— because there is a *lot* of material now out there—and boy, are they *super* detailed. TMI does not begin to cut it. Again, one of the storytellers said she realized she was on the cusp of *the change* because she began to feel 'not like herself'. A sentiment noticeably repeated by so many others. But how does that translate for those who maybe never felt like they fit in their skin? Who were always a little awkward or unsteady? Who never quite felt like other people? How then would someone who always felt distinct be able to tell if they were going through something *new* that was physiological? Anxiety? Depression? Sleepless nights? Hot sweats? All that can make a girl feel like she did at the height of puberty. Or perhaps like falling in love for the first time and getting your heart broken. That overwhelming sense of dread where you question the very reason for your existence. Such angst reappearing in your forties can seem like a visit from an old friend.

Speaking of old friends, we ended our call feeling encouraged and enriched, but oh how I wish I had learned to appreciate things sooner. All the places I'd swung through and the people I'd encountered. All the things I'd seen and the stories I'd heard. I wish I had danced more, and sang more, and feasted. And took steps forward when I held myself back too frightened to leap. I wish I had *dared* . . . when I was diminished by my own insecurities.

Maybe then I could now look back at my younger self without feeling just that little bit—

—betrayed.

19 July

A Postcard from New York

It's all light and shadow. Bleeding into each other in small, brusque brushstrokes on a black canvas. Suspended in the tension between being . . . and possibility. Night in New York.

From how this evening strikes me, you would think I'd never seen buildings in clusters before. I have, of course, but it's never quite been this claustrophobic. There's hardly a clear view of the sky. And yet, I am not gasping for air.

Seeing the city from this twenty-ninth-floor balcony, smack in the middle of it, is very different from being on the ground. It's as if I am cradled among the skyscrapers. All light and shadow myself. I bleed into the evening just as it bleeds into me. (Goodness, what is with this relentlessly sanguineous imagery?) The night is pulsating, and here I am at the centre of the cyclone. I am nothing and everything at once. *Everything.* It's a whirl of energy. No skin, no containers, no limits. Tonight, I am part of the force that thrums through this city. In constant motion. In constant motion . . . *Alive.*

A hornet's nest.

This is also what my head feels like right now. A hornet's nest. A twenty-first century Monet painting. Dots and dashes. Ones and Zeros. Buzzing with electricity. Pulsing, pregnant brushstrokes seemingly strewn haphazardly on a canvas. I am still too close to it to see the full image, slowly working my way through squiggles and slashes that have yet to become fully formed shapes. Lost in a vibrating, vibrant jungle of solfège syllables. A shambolic stave of noise. Rising and falling seemingly without meter or rhyme. But I have no doubt it will play a symphony . . . once I am ready to hear it. For now, I am floating on a sheet of scattered notes. Fully expecting the waves to take me to shore.

Take me to shore.

Eventually.

For now, I must live in the *float*. I had always thought I needed space. An open view. A panorama. The sea . . . a garden . . . anything that didn't crowd me. But I was wrong and I guess it is right that I am here. In Manhattan. A city I failed to appreciate before. Now, the bleeding, bustling metropolis is a reflection of where I'm at . . . who I am at this moment.

Moment. I am living in the moment. Something I learned on the job. Having to focus on what's happening in front of you keeps you from disappearing into your head, from worrying about the future or bemoaning the past. The work—the *news*—kept me in the moment. And I see now that was not a bad thing. But I also wonder in all that 'being present', where was I? A viewer alongside everyone else—just closer. Did it make the world any more real for me? And if not—what would that mean? And of what consequence if I don't recall much of it? And what about you who may have been watching . . . there was very little about the person who was showing it to you. Did you see me? In all the reality I was trying to show you—did you feel the need to see me?

In the black and white of life's jagged edges, how do we behave as if it's all right that only some people are privy to the light? Maybe it's time we take a step back from our rat races and ask ourselves different questions. The *why* questions. Why are things as they are? Why is everyone so obsessed with the spotlight? Why do people do what they do? And why do I want what I think I want? What for? What for? What for? And what do I expect at the end of all this? Does it even matter? Does any of it matter?

So I told a few stories, I went on a few journeys, and I bled a little on the page . . . but what does any of it matter?

Word Count

Writing this seemed like a good idea in the beginning. I remember exactly where I was when this was 'birthed'— working on the manuscript for a novel, *Calle Sombra*, at my late parents' house. I alternated between clearing out their closets, sorting through every nook and cranny of the forty-year-old, well-loved and lived-in home, and editing the novel's manuscript. For that, I would sit at a table in the empty porch staring out at the breezy garden. Once lush and full of flowers, what remained seemed sad and sullen . . . despite being dappled in gold by the sun dripping in through the dense leaves of the old mango tree that had shaded our childhood. It always broke my heart. When it became too much, as it often did, a change of pace demanded acquiescence. Almost automatically, I opened a new document on my laptop and just started writing. Words poured out as if they were set loose and needed to run free. As if I had been choking and this was a sudden exhalation. Essay after essay came together on the page. And they all seemed to be existential cries for . . . something. I only shut the document down when I had nothing left to say. At least for that afternoon. I put it all aside—including the existential angst—and returned to what needed doing. The *Sombra* edit and the editing of my family home. It was not an easy time.

A long while later, I rediscovered the Word document I had created that afternoon, full of musings and reflections. Date and timestamped. They were like little presents to myself. Digital messages in a virtual bottle. A sort of word dump from when my head needed a breather from the fictional world I was immersed in during the *Sombra* edit. I didn't necessarily always feel the same as I had when I started the document, but I find that sometimes, going over what I've written helps me both understand and appreciate the journey.

I have always kept a journal—for as long as I can remember. But the older I got, the less I felt the need to work through my feelings and thoughts by putting them down on the page. I was once quite chatty, but silence had become a friend, and I learned to just sit and let things wash over me. I also noticed that the less troubled or anxious I was, the less I felt compelled to journal. But when the urge arose, I still left myself little notes in all sorts of 'places'. Text messages to myself. Emails in my draft box. Scribbles on the back of receipts. A line or two if I felt bad or if a thought crossed my mind that I wanted to later re-examine. (For example, I just found this scribbled on a slip of paper: *It is no coincidence that 'mind' and 'mined' sound the same.*) I was always *mining* my thoughts for the right questions to ask the Universe. I never thought the answers might lay within me—but I believed that if I silenced myself enough, I would hear them come.

Well, wouldn't you know it, here I am—after proposing this idea to my publisher—now needing to meet a deadline and unable to find any words that I feel make a difference.

I look around me now and all I feel . . . is silence.

Fortune Smiles · · · on Someone Else

Did you know that nearly half of the people born between 1965 and 1980 are unmarried? Nearly *half!* That's around 500 million people. No generation before it has been quite as 'single'. And depending on who you ask, that is either terribly unfortunate or quite the opposite. The other day, a woman in her late sixties commented on a viral social media post that lucky are those who have not had to *suffer* through a partner. She didn't seem to realize that her partner's relatives (i.e., the person who showed me the post) could see her statement. But, then again, according to said relative, considering who this woman married, no one could fault her the sentiment.

The older I get, the more I realize that there are many like this unsuspecting woman for whom *adulting* means needing to compromise daily on everything from what to watch on TV to who uses the toilet first, what groceries to buy, and what colour couch to own. Meanwhile, those living by themselves can choose what they want for dinner—or perhaps skip the meal entirely. These singletons can opt not to shower or decide not to get out of bed in the morning. In comparison, such solitude and independence can seem a more peaceful life . . . no? Especially when juxtaposed with this rather colourful couple I met recently who are in their seventies. They go everywhere together and also share an office. They have children, grandchildren, a coterie of pets, and multiple homes. They've been together since they were in their twenties and though clearly devoted to each other, they insist there is such a thing as *too much* togetherness. Everyone within earshot who heard them agreed on that. And then they proceeded to do what they've become known for in their circles—bicker as if it were going out of style or would improve their health. Go figure. How many times have we seen the trope of the constantly feuding couple on TV? I mean, if you struggle to agree on things—or worse, actively dislike each other—why stay together? But it seems many of the older generation have felt the need to remain married despite the option to divorce. Better the devil you know? Or maybe they believe the alternative would send them straight to hell. (For the non-religious: yes, it's a thing.) In most faith-, or rather, religion-based societies, marriage between a man and a woman has long been seen as the cornerstone of the community. All social order rests on this. You couple up, stay together through thick and thin—no matter the mistresses, the lies, or the abuse—and you keep your mouth shut. At least about certain things. That's how stability—or the semblance of it—is maintained. And stability inevitably means conformity. Maybe that's why so many in succeeding generations have raged against it? Who knows.

Most people I know who are my age have remained unencumbered. Whether by choice or otherwise. Is it perhaps in our DNA? Is it born of a desire to remain true to ourselves and uncompromising? Or perhaps a need to not be like the generation before? Has a search for our own identities led to an inability to make space for someone else? In our drive to be our own heroes . . . have we created our own tragedies? I just read an article about the Gen X actor Bradley Cooper saying he wouldn't be alive if not for his daughter, crediting his DNA for showing him there's something more important than himself. He said that through the turbulence of his life, parenthood anchors him—and maybe there's the rub.

Maybe it's the definition of commitment that has changed.

#

Doing the dishes the other day, I received a message on social media from an acquaintance in near tears. They'd seen one of my posts and it sent them spinning. That they reached out took me by surprise. But I suppose it is sometimes easier to speak your truth to a stranger, which is why the anonymity of social media communities can offer such solace.

Unlike Bradley Cooper, this person was feeling trapped in their life—as a parent and a spouse. Lost in someone else's plan. Swept up and away by a torrent of what they called 'suddenly unfamiliar' realities. They were taken over by reflections they hadn't previously considered. Who were they in the dreams of their children? Who were they in the life goals of their spouse? Were they now going to be simply defined as so and-so's other half? They felt like half a person. This was a strong individual long in control of their life—what changed? Having a partner? How then do you find the balance between staying sane and staying married? What do you do when your life feels like it is no longer your own?

When your life feels like it isn't your own . . .

I often felt like that when I was on the news treadmill. Running from one assignment to the next. It gave me a purpose but when that stopped, so did my reason for being. The reason to get up in the morning. The purpose. The meaning. The meaning. The *meaning*.

How small I became to think that all I was was down to the *job* I had married. So, who was I after I divorced the network? I had disassociated myself from all the letters that had defined me—the various combinations of G, M, A, B, S, C, N, L, J, Z, E, and R. Without any of it, what was the point of my existence?

I even went so far as to search online for the meaning of life. Just out of curiosity. I wanted to know what answers the digital sphere might provide. There were prayer websites, tarot sites, angel messaging pages, psychic contact forms, rune readings, et cetera, et cetera, et cetera. You name it—I stumbled upon it. All in an attempt to find some meaning. ONLINE! How inane! I went from taking long walks and breathing in the ocean air to scanning/trawling through the tides of the interweb. The intangible waves of the WWW. Let me tell you—the answer is not there.

I've gotten this far and now I don't even recall what the question was. We were speaking on commitment, were we not? About how . . . maybe what has changed is our definition of it. Who said it was limited to a promise we make to another person? Be it a partner or a child? What about also being true to oneself? Sometimes, those truths, those commitments intersect. And whether that is a matter of good or ill fortune is, again, all down to perspective.

Front Row

I can't recall when I first heard it being referred to as the front row, but I think it may have been when my parents lost a number of their friends within a short span of time. 'We're next in line,' one of them said. 'Up front now . . .' The generation before them had gone and they were now within sight of death.

Well, this is not a joyous way to start this chapter. But I am sure you see where I am heading. Although people these days are living longer, fuller lives, those in my age group are quickly moving up to the front row. I had childhood friends pass away while we were still in school, and a few more before we even hit our forties. I get now why it's said of people dying in their forties that they're so young—they are! I just didn't see that until I got there.

Now, I know people younger than me dealing with grave illnesses and fighting for their lives . . . not having the space to question why. It's not as if the answer to that would even matter.

I don't like being in the front row. It's taken away my hope and my desire to dream or think there may be more left to live. All I see from here are the heavy curtains waiting to fall . . . as I struggle to get back outside the theatre where life is waiting.

WHO CARES?

Merienda with a Side of Myopia

I live next door to someone I've known since I was thirteen. We started out as rivals, but somehow ended up friends. Go figure. She has multiple jobs and a multitude of children. We don't see each other that often. Literally across the street and we maybe meet up twice a year. Maybe.

One day soon after the cusp of the new year was the first of those times. We had agreed to meet for merienda, a light afternoon snack, in a modest café near her office in a busy area between her meetings. No time for long lunches or dinners, just a rushed window from 4.30 to 6 p.m. There could be no running late or being too early. When you hit a certain age, you realize time is a precious commodity. Also increasingly precious is one's memory. It's barely a week since that I write this, but I can't even recall what I wore. Most days I just throw something on to make sure I don't shock people by being naked. I think I may have had a dress on—or rather, a duster that could pass for a dress—and I likely wore earrings, just to feel a tad more put together. No make-up though—that would've been too much effort for a 'breezy' afternoon merienda. At least as far as I was concerned.

I got to the café early and sat near the back corner by the floor-to-ceiling glass pane and a giant stand fan. It was the coolest spot in the place. And it also, thankfully, put the wall with the large mirror behind me. (Don't you just hate having your reflection look back at you when you're eating? Or when you're doing any other thing at all? No? Just me then?) Anyway . . .

At the designated time, I got a text from my friend to say she was in the lift on her way to the café. She was always punctual or at least efficient about letting you know if she was going to be late—though it was barely three minutes past the agreed appointment.

She dashed in, as elegantly as she does, wearing tan-coloured mules like ones I had seen on my mother and a business-y striped dress that had been starched and pressed. Since our last meeting (lives across the street remember?), her shiny black hair had been chanced upon by a few sophisticated greys. Her eye make-up—a constant since we were teens—was just enough to make her not look pale. She was spotless, as always, and well turned out—(no duster for her!)—and she looked her age. A commanding, dignified woman. And yet, to me, she also looked just like she did in high school. Back when there wasn't so much of a divide between us. We wore similar clothes then, similar shoes, and kept our hair in sort of the same fashion. Now, I just feel like the awkward cousin you don't invite to your debut.

She gracefully took her seat and ordered an Americano—one shot of espresso, decaf—because she had a dinner to get to after and didn't want to eat beforehand. I, on the other hand, ordered a brimming mug of hot chocolate and a fluffy, buttery, three-cheese sweet bread to dunk into it.

We talked about cholesterol, liver functions, and chest pains. This was followed by a discussion on sugar levels and high blood pressure. How odd it is that one can go from being anaemic when younger to needing medication to calm down.

We spoke of common acquaintances who have had strokes, organ transplants, or kidney issues. So and so was widowed, so and so needed stents. Did you hear about so and so who had to take on the care of her elderly parents? They're like children now after being so in control.

We considered which might be the better option—having parents pass away before they get to that stage (as ours had), or having them around longer regardless of their mental faculties? There is no right answer to that question.

And that is what we realized—there are no 'right answers' to life's biggest questions. Only what works for each of us. And that won't be the same across the board. What is right for her won't necessarily be so for me. Despite what we once might have had in common.

In that brief period between 4.30 and 6 p.m., we spoke in the shorthand language of long-time friends, without once mentioning who might have gained weight or gathered wrinkles. We talked vaguely of our shared past and more clearly of the present, though our paths through the years have diverged. Life has not always been kind, but somehow, when it mattered, we each showed up for the other. I never once wondered what she saw when she looked at me all these decades later, certain that I was still the same thirteen-year-old girl.

As I tried to keep the hot chocolate from dripping on my duster/dress, I asked her what the most important thing getting older has taught her. She passed me a napkin, and without stopping for breath, she said: 'Acceptance.'

She's right. The older you are, the faster you're able to reconcile things and move on. From disappointments, disillusion, and dejections. You spend less time questioning every decision, trusting that things will work out however they work out and you will manage regardless. As you age, there is less raging against the world and more collaboration. Just like we went from rivals to friends.

Of course, what we thought was important in high school is clearly no longer the same at midlife, and she noted there was now acceptance of the things she'd never understand.

And though our eyesight is no longer as it was when we were younger, we perhaps see things clearer than we had before. Even if we might need various pairs of lenses to do so.

As expected, 6 p.m. arrived faster than we would've wanted. My friend's Americano remained mostly untouched, while my mug was practically wiped clean of any trace of chocolate. Neither of us had once looked out the glass panel or glanced in the direction of the mirror.

We rose together to say goodbye, making perfunctory arrangements for our next encounter. She tucked away the glasses she'd used to read the menu, and I switched out mine for the pair I would need to make my way home. As I put them on, she dashed for the door as breezily as she'd come, a familiar but unrecognizable woman in her adult striped suit and grown-up shoes.

I Remember the Girl

A modest, red brick terraced house not far from the Thames and the cultural heart of London. I remember every corner, every tile, every nook. The walls were a pale cornsilk yellow, and the carpet was beige, covering all three storeys and the flights of stairs. The winding banister was white as were the door frames. There were three bedrooms, a lounge, a single car garage that we used for storage and a pocket garden by the kitchen with a small, paved area surrounded by tropical plants. We left the back doors open on many balmy afternoons as we enjoyed our evening repast and a catch up. This place is still the repository of many of my happiest memories as an 'adult'. From the get-go, I couldn't believe my luck. (Those were the days when I instinctively believed it was on my side.) The rent was surprisingly cheap for London, but it did take half my scholarship's meagre monthly stipend. So, it was either food and my daily needs or this wonderful place to call a home. No brainer. I chose the home.

And no regrets. It was worth it. I unintentionally lost a **lot** of weight, but for five years—on the same rent—I lived happily in this house with two others who were also transplants to the British capital. People only moved out when they had to relocate abroad. But we were like a sorority—or what I might imagine one to be. A bond was forged, and whenever those who had left came back for a visit, they stayed with those of us still at the house.

We all became fast friends and remain so to this day, more than two decades later.

Gosh, I miss being that young. When nights could be spent talking endlessly about where we wanted to be and how we saw our lives panning out. When everything felt possible and we knew that where we were at was a moment of *transition*. London, in that sense, felt suspended in time. A place we came to to discover who we were and test our boundaries. Did you also go through a similar period? I am sure we were not the only ones to pass through such a stage. We were small town kids who had big dreams in this big city. And we were happy to keep our noses to the ground doing what seemed to be menial jobs because we saw them as stepping stones to larger platforms. We believed we could do it all, so long as we worked hard and kept looking to the stars.

Looking back now, life hasn't quite gone the way we might have hoped, but I think none of us can say that things didn't 'work out'. Somehow. We made do and rose to unexpected occasions. But I won't pretend there haven't been frustration and some upset along the way. Like when things didn't quite go to plan. Or that unshakeable feeling that you just watched other lives go past . . . like you were simply a witness to the ebb and flow of someone else's dreams-come-true while sitting on the riverbank being shat on by birds.

We were going to open a sandwich shop along the Thames and write the next bestselling phenomenon. We were going to form an acoustic group called Sahara Summer and live in a giant house with bay windows overlooking a sprawling lawn.

There is sadness, there is guilt, there is . . . I suppose . . . some disappointment. There is envy at the innocence and certainty of youth.

How I remember that girl with stars in her eyes who dreamed those dreams, and oh how I wish I still saw her in the mirror.

WHAT DO I REALLY WANT?

Imaginary Playmates

Should someone ask you what you *really* want—would you have an answer? I sort of thought I did. But then, that came and went, and now I'm . . . stuck. Without an updated response to such a crucial question. I can't recall who it was that pointed out that it is the *wanting,* the need to *create* or go *in pursuit* of something that keeps us going. People are *desire* in search of fulfilment. Without that, do we lose our lust for life?

Most children go through a phase of having imaginary friends, a vital part—according to the experts—of their development. It offers a 'safe space' to practice social interaction, express emotions, and boost independence. But I never had such playmates. Instead, I wrote. That's what I did. I took great pleasure in exploring the many ways words could be strung together to capture an emotion or create a scene. They kept me company, and the page was where I exercised many imagined social interactions. I had notebooks in all sorts of sizes covered in plastic and plastered with stickers. Some had drawings all over them or black-and-white photocopied images of John F. Kennedy on the cover. Why? Because I was obsessed with him as a child. I had seen the TV miniseries *Kennedy* that starred Martin Sheen as JFK, and the obsession was born. In the pages of this one special JFK notebook was a collection of words I held dearest. It was like my secret journal. Only it wasn't. It wasn't a record of daily events or a collection of personal confessions. Everything in it was made up or born from a fascination with something else outside of me. The entries always either shone a light on a subject I was trying to understand or one I appreciated.

In this secret non-journal, I once wrote a poem about ice cream using the names of all the different kinds made by the lone local ice cream maker. I managed rhyme and verse about Upside Down icicles, Mango Bangos, and chocolate Twin Popsies. I also wrote about forests I'd never seen and castles I'd only imagined. Much of it was a creative exercise, but there were also entries prompted by real life tragedies. A neighbour had lost their children in a car crash and those deaths stayed with me a good number of years. Then I wrote about a father serving in the US army and dying in Vietnam. What did I know about that? Absolutely nothing. But I could see it clearly in my mind. Through a filtered, slow-motion lens of sadness and grief. So I set it in the States . . . in the fall. Why? Because fall colours are sombre and sentimental, colours that can break your heart. And there was no fall in the tropics where I lived. So, of course, the story had to be set in the States. Looking back now, I think I just wanted to write about the violence of losing a parent.

I wrote it on my mother's new electric typewriter. Boy, was that a treat. An electric typewriter! It was red. With a digital screen where the ribbons used to be on older models. But this swishy electric typewriter couldn't replace my secret 'non-journal'. And when I am feeling most raw and vulnerable, I still write by hand. It keeps me closer to the truths I may not be able to say but can feel. It keeps me more rooted in the things I might not be conscious of but know deep in my gut.

My literature teacher loved that story. It made her cry. I think because it reminded her of her own father who was a doctor in the guerrilla movement during the Second World War. He survived the war but not a heart attack decades later. Anything that reminded my teacher of him made her weep. He was her parent. I should've realized then how such deaths turn a life upside down . . . but I hadn't a clue.

How did I know this about my teacher? She was also my mother. But that's another story. Some might think that having your mother as your teacher is a sweet deal, that it would make you the teacher's pet, but believe me it was quite the opposite. My mother was one of the—no—my mother was *the* most upright person I have ever met. There was no way she was going to be seen to be favouring her daughter. In fact, she was admittedly harder on me than any of her other students. She also expected more of me. She always strove to be fair, but there was often a different set of rules where her own children were concerned. They were always more rigid. I guess in some universes, parents also expect their kids to be perfect and not just vice versa.

So yes, my mother was the woman responsible for developing in me a love of storytelling. Both by giving me a fairly boring (read: safe and happy) childhood where I had to make my own excitement and then by teaching me the classic stories of the world in my high school literature classes.

Thinking about it now, damn right, I was lucky. Even my passion in life is born of my mother. That gave me a sort of blueprint to follow or veer away from, which I suppose is what all progenitors offer—a legacy to live up to or leave behind.

Funnily, as much as she instilled in me a love for the word, I don't actually recall her ever reading to my siblings and me while we were growing up, and she never regaled us with stories about her own childhood. She never did like talking about herself, my mother. Always preferring to be a *pointer* instead. To lead you to look somewhere else. Like a magician with a sleight of hand, my mom was always shoving books in our direction, telling us to read, read, read. We didn't all have to read the same books nor discuss what we read with her. In that sense, I suppose,

I gleaned that it was meant to be a solitary experience. That the Word was to be delved into alone.

To me, reading didn't feel like something that *connected* people . . . but was a special gift that showed you how much of the world still lay beyond the safety of your comfort zone.

I have reached a point though where I feel I have read as much as I can currently handle, and the word—once familiar— has become estranged. My notebooks are empty, and my imagined wants have waned.

I had always been happiest in the company of words, but any solace they once offered has fled my pen.

UnLinkAble

Why am I still on LinkedIn? You know the one, the social media platform meant to connect 'professionals'. I can't recall when I set up my account—likely while I was still gainfully employed—or for what reason, but now that I don't have a 'proper' job, it taunts me in a way I never expected. Stupidly, I also downloaded the app onto my phone, so it can torment me any time, day or night, without need of going through the tedious process of opening up a laptop to log on to the website. How utterly convenient. I can just look at this wee unassuming app on my phone and be reminded 24/7 of how under-accomplished I am. Comparatively speaking. Seeing the app users' posts can't help but make me feel like I've had a terribly crappy career. Which certainly means that somewhere along the line, I must've failed. Unlike every other Tom, Mark, and Elizabeth, I am not a multi-awarded, multifaceted, hyper-achieving CEO or tech leader or entrepreneurial self-made billionaire. I am not an *eminent* international journalist nor am I an overly educated, deeply determined humanitarian saving the world from itself. I am not performing groundbreaking surgeries, discovering medical marvels, or coming up with cures for incurable illnesses. Oh, and let's not forget the peace brokers, the global politicians, and the professional personalities. Those who have made a living out of being the grandest, loudest versions of themselves. They give insightful, encouraging TED talks, send out newsletters, keep a blog, and write books upon how-to books about their immeasurable successes. I am not any of that, but everyone else on the website/platform seems to fall into one or a number of those categories.

Since I left my 'proper' job, this professionals' networking site that serves up constant reminders of how much I have underachieved, has done nothing more than depress me. It's unsettling and has become a source of anxiety. Sure, when I was employed, I had things to post about, but who had time then? Then I walked away from that 'important' career, thinking I would eventually land back on my feet and have other things to post about. But months passed and I had little to share. The app kept pinging with other people's notifications, and I felt like a ghost, a lurker, on this platform for achievements. I was but the audience for the boasts of successful people. Why again did I walk away from the job last listed on my profile? For peace of mind? To *reorient* myself? To take a breather? What b*ll*cks! How dare I? I was not protecting the planet from poachers, polluters, or pirates. I was not mediating geopolitical disagreements or building homes for impoverished communities in far flung regions. What did I need a 'break' from? I hadn't done anything *important*. Every time I got a notification of someone or other accomplishing yet another noble, heroic feat, I was reminded of my smallness. The *in*-consequence of my existence. Is this what the app was meant for? To push its users into questioning their worth? To measure the value they contribute to society? To re-examine their life choices? Because that is what it has led me to do. Three decades I worked my ass off to 'cover the news', to be on 'the frontline of history' and stand witness, to tell the stories that would otherwise go unheard or be overlooked—and for what? For much of my work to disappear into the ether. For me as an individual to also be overlooked and forgotten. But then again, I never did like the spotlight. I never enjoyed being looked at, which was why I settled easily into telling other people's stories in the first place. So, it shouldn't have bothered me that no one seemed to care when I stopped covering the news, right? But it did. Bother me. It made me feel ineffect/ive/ual. Like everything I worked tirelessly to put out there was meaningless and fleeting. We *all* worked so hard on these twenty-four-hour news cycles—and it does feel like ultimately, no one cares.

A senior reporter I worked with a long time ago told me that journalists are a dime a dozen. They come and go, and only a handful are remembered or make a difference.

'We can't all be Amanpour,' she told me without any rancour or envy, referring to the highest paid journalist around, 'and that's okay. We have to keep in mind that that's not why we became reporters. Right? At the end of the day, we just wanted to get out there and tell stories.' It was a sobering reminder.

These days, if I go on any social media platform and trawl (not troll) through its endless feed, it is packed with multitudes telling stories. And everyone—even children—is hyperaware that they're *storytellers*. Beyond that, they're all *creating* 'content'. And this, mind you, is a recognized profession to hype up on your LinkedIn profile. 'Content creator'. And many content creators are reaping a fortune from their self-propelled enterprises. My time reporting the news wasn't quite like that, though there are now more and more self-employed, aka freelance or *independent* journalists. A few of them are unabashedly self-proclaimed and putting material out there as self-created content. In this morass of all these selves, any voice I might have is just one more drop in a boundless ocean. The most I can hope for these days is that any stories I am moved to tell will find their audience . . . and the rest, well, anything above that, would be a bonus.

#

Update: I have turned off my LinkedIn notifications. This way, I am no longer subjected to any more announcements of people's bravura. But somehow, I can't yet bring myself to delete the app entirely. Perhaps I am still thinking it may be my last lifeline to getting back on the job market. To finding some sort of relevance. And I did try. Sent a bunch of applications for jobs that were not quite right because, frankly, I didn't know what a 'retired' journalist might be good for. I could teach, but nothing permanent has panned out. I could write regularly for an online site, but as I mentioned earlier, seems no one's interested in what I might have to say. I could manage a newsroom, but back-room execs seem to have trouble imagining a 'field person' calling the shots and making decisions from behind a desk. Which is silly considering field people have to become adept at making important, quick-fire—sometimes life or death—decisions. Saying we function under pressure is an understatement. Every day, on every assignment, that is the grind. It is routine to make a rapid assessment, deliberate thoughtfully on what information is available, trust your gut, often think out of the box, and deliver. Skills that would be useful anywhere. In all that, I never once thought to post about it on LinkedIn. I never thought to *celebrate* the necessary achievements of my modest career. And maybe that has been my mistake?

The other day, I reconnected with my former news editor on a video call arranged by his assistant. He didn't have an assistant when we first worked together years earlier.

Anyway, it had been posted on LinkedIn that this news editor-turned-exec had leapfrogged several countries, held key jobs in various networks, and was now in the mecca of the profession—the U-S-A. Despite many notable and lauded global organizations, working in the US is still frequently considered the pinnacle of a news person's career. There are journalists who give up their tracks on international networks to join one of the 'Big Three' in 'America'. The major media employers who have seen the likes of broadcasting legends such as Walter Cronkite, Ted Koppel, and Jane Pauley. Why? Bigger bucks perhaps? A chance to become a news 'personality' with a whiff of power? If you're famous in the States, you're a celebrity everywhere, right? You can command your price and dictate the rules? Who knows for sure why the US market is still the goal for many? Each person will surely have their own reasons.

So, anyway, I was told by another former colleague that the network our old news manager was working with was looking to hire, and since here was someone who knew my work, I thought that I might actually get a shot at a job.

Full disclosure: I didn't necessarily want to be in a newsroom full time, but despite years 'on sabbatical', I still didn't know where else to go. I had yet to find my 'secondary dream', if you will. So maybe, I considered, this is what I was meant for. Surely this was why, after a rather long break to mull things over, I was still lost? It must be time—I thought—to buckle back down and return to the news. (Can you believe it? 'Middle-aged' and still so indecisive.)

I sent him a message on LinkedIn (where else?), and he asked for my updated CV. We then set a call (with the help of his assistant), and eventually had a long chat that was honestly like a much-needed therapy session (without a fee!). I had never been so happy to speak to a former manager. His demeanour and his generosity reminded me why he must've gone as far as he had in his career. He had a quiet authority to him and invited— not commanded—respect. He asked all the right questions, was insightful and incisive, and very courteously and kindly told me that my CV sucked. Not because my career highlights were unimpressive but because I hadn't geared their descriptions to the right—i.e., American—audience. He was aware of what

I could do and where I had been, but it seems I hadn't presented my professional milestones in a way that would be understood by hiring mangers focused on a domestic market and not looking to appreciate international stories. I hadn't written my CV in terms of what I could contribute to their goals or how I might best serve their needs, only stressing old stories that read like an outdated list of headlines. It failed to highlight any of my skills and was only a chronological record of my employers. It was my first time hearing this, and it was such a EUREKA moment. *Of course!* Suddenly, it all made sense.

This was it in a nutshell—my LinkedIn issue. No wonder I never got a second look from hiring execs. I am not saying I have been unemployed in the years since I left on-air reporting, but with all the CVs I'd sent out and messages I had written, this professional networking site has not actually got me any work. I should have considered myself a commodity to be sold to a buying audience, but I didn't know how to angle myself according to a market.

Ping!—There it is again. Another notification. Scores of people on this professional site celebrating everything from a promotion to a public speaking engagement. And everyone seems to be speaking publicly. Makes you wonder with all the 'speakers' if there's anyone still actually *listening*. With so many successes, how can there be room for any more plaudits? One connection won a global award, while another got a seven-figure deal for a yet-to-be-written book. In such an arena, how can one hope to stand out? Never mind stand out, it's tough to even figure out how to just stand *among*.

Ping!—It may be time to delete the app . . . but I still can't bring myself to do it. It's as if staying on the site is proof that I still count, even though I know it is all a lie. It is all a lie—to fool myself into thinking I still have a professional profile and to fool others into believing it too. This whole exercise has made me feel *less than.* So thank goodness for that one conversation with my old news manager. It has at least reminded me of who I am—unapologetically unsure but undaunted.

Ping!

This app has got to go. I hate it. It has made me hate where I am at. All because I don't know how to describe what I do—or who I am—on a bloody professional networking site!

Another List

Things I regret:

- Not spending more time with family

Frequencies and Mantras: Gen X in a DeGENerate World

Over the years, there was a mantra I heard a lot: 'You're so lucky.' *You're so lucky.* You're so lucky. You're so lucky. Yes, I am intentionally writing it four times for emphasis. People thought me incredibly fortunate to be 'doing' what I was 'doing'— and I am not suggesting that they were wrong. In case you're reading this chapter before preceding ones, what I was *doing* was covering the news. I *was* a journalist. I was a journalist for so long that when I stopped doing the work, I lost sight of who I was. I no longer knew how to define myself. If I wasn't a journalist anymore, then who was I? What was the point of me? What was my value? I know this isn't a feeling unique to me. People often feel lost when they face an ending with no clear view of the next chapter. What we might later recognize as a turning point could in the moment just very well have us spinning.

I lived out of a suitcase for decades, travelled to and fro to the point of whiplash, and met so many interesting people often when they were living through their worst. No day was the same. 'How exciting!' I was often told. 'You get to see everything first-hand. All the *important* stuff.'

Yes, certainly. But in so doing, I took a ringside seat to my own life. My own reality seemed to go on *outside* of me. Or off tangent from me. I never quite knew if I was coming or going. More often than not, it was both at the same time. It's easy to understand why so many journalists have nervous breakdowns. But of course, they're not the only ones who do. And that feeling of *watching* your life go by is not unusual. I'm sure our obsession with the virtual world has contributed to that sense of not being in control. Of feeling a little lost and displaced.

Why is it that so many people think the lives of others are more fulfilling or worthwhile than their own? Instead of jousting with envy, we should be learning to appreciate where we're at and what we've got. In this age of the 'selfie'—the self-promotion, the self-importance, the narcissism—you would think that true self-appreciation would be automatic, but it isn't. What there is is a lot of self-doubt. There is something to be said about those who feel the need to show off on social media perhaps because they actually feel so small. It's almost as if they think that if they don't exist online, they don't exist at all. So, we've cultivated a culture full of sham wizards in a one-dimensional world, all digital smoke and mirrors to hide our most painful truths. In this civilized age of global communication, we've just developed more high-tech ways to hide the emptiness.

Supernova

It was a surprising morning. After a night that I mostly slept through, I awoke with little to no pain anywhere in my body. That's enough to put me on the right side of the bed, as it were, as I arise. On mornings like this one—rare and few they are—I almost feel like myself again. As if I still have an abundance of adventures ahead of me and am not actually being counted down to an expiration date. As if I am not drowning in a torrent of worries and can still float along on uncharted journeys. As if I am still in the throes of youth and everything is yet to be discovered. *As if . . . as if . . . as if . . .* Sigh.

But then, I don't know, one thing went wrong and then another. Small things really, nothing major. Like the breakfast order arriving late and cold, a scheduled meeting inexplicably postponed, and draft scripts submitted to me for editing needing more help than should be required. See? Nothing major. I had to wrack my brain to even recall most of that now to write it down. But small things can sometimes reverberate like a supernova. Especially these days. So what began as a bright and joyful morning unexpectedly and immediately escalated to a raging storm. I wasn't sure if I was about to scream in anger and frustration or burst into tears from a sudden feeling of hopelessness. Frankly, it felt like all of those emotions rolled into one large chaotic unstable ball. I didn't know where or how to let these powerful feelings flow. I shuddered inside as I was about to explode from the sheer force of the energy I was needing to bottle up. If I yelled out of the blue, I would seem slightly mad. And if I broke down and sobbed, well that would have been no better. And try explaining where you're at to the people around you. It's near impossible when you're so lost in the tide and just trying to keep from drowning. *Lie back, daughter,* I recall a poem my mother taught me . . . *lie gently and wide to the light-year stars* . . . when the thrash to your island gets too much. *Lie back, and the sea will hold.*

That poem by Philip Booth has always been a comfort, but sometimes, even the lying back takes more strength than I can muster. And on those days—quite like the one that began this entry—I wonder what it would be like if I just turned my head into the waves and let it hold me.

Sometimes, it all feels a tad too much and I can't breathe. And though my doctor has told me my hormones are all over the place at the moment, I am not quite sure what that's supposed to tell me. That what I am feeling isn't real? That I am to let all this *guck* just wash over me? That I am to hold on to what exactly while I am thrashed around by unending tides? I often feel like I am drowning—

Many of the articles I have read lately tell me I am not alone. That 70 per cent of women my age feel the same. Is that true? Who knows! But it could be. It *seems* so. So, what do we do? Do we hold on to each other for buoyancy? For company and sympathy? It would help, but we must know that our journeys through midlife are distinct and different . . .

I woke up today with such hope that maybe somewhere in this misery I was still myself, instead, I found I was cast overboard with a rock tied to my feet.

It is hard work to remain as positive and optimistic as required in this 'woke' age of the politically correct and the entitled 'enlightened'. And sometimes, I just can't do it anymore.

Boom.

Supernova.

WHAT COULD I HAVE DONE DIFFERENTLY?

FRIDAYS  FREEDOM

FINALLY

aka

F*ck it!

Golden Girls

When I was growing up, fifty looked like a white-maned Bea Arthur living without a partner in a bungalow with other women of the same age and her eighty-year-old mother, whom we couldn't believe was even still alive! Now, women in their fifties look like Sarah Jessica Parker playing Carrie Bradshaw and Jennifer Aniston playing, well, anything. They're fashion icons, rock stars on world tours, and entrepreneurs at the peak of their careers. And women in their eighties? They're running marathons, presiding over courts, and starring in hit TV shows that have them doing physical comedy and sleeping around!

It's not that women have drastically changed—but maybe mindsets have? With so much attention put on health and lifestyle choices, people have been taking better care of themselves. And when you stop feeling 'old', you begin to see that there is more of life ahead than you might have expected. So, a step at a time, you approach it with optimism and excited anticipation instead of fear and dread.

They keep saying 'age is just a number', and maybe people these days are redefining what those numbers mean. They are not as set in stone as we might have thought.

In France, perceptions of 'middle age' have evolved to where sixty is apparently the new forty. Make of that what you will. But I am told that despite being the age of retirement, sixty is also taken to be the point at which people can start afresh. The shackles of a job are gone, and they can finally go full throttle into a renaissance.

'I can't wait to hit sixty,' a dear friend confided the other day. 'I felt so free the moment I turned fifty that I can just imagine how utterly fab it will be at sixty to not give a toss about anything.'

Along with her self-confidence, there's a sense of freedom. That at sixty the last thing she will be is confined to a home for the elderly. 'It's a different world, dear Marga . . .' she chuckled.

We are also not ageing alone. In this digital era of social media, we are constantly barraged with the thoughts of the world every second of the day. And there is no escaping specialized 'communities', even age-related ones. There are senior chats and travel groups aside from book clubs. Can we still claim to have an original idea that hasn't been influenced by something or other we've seen in a five-second video somewhere? It's like living in a virtual bungalow with all your chattiest virtual 'friends', as well as some cross-generational representatives who pay no heed to boundaries.

When I was growing up, I always thought the world *belonged* to the adults. They ran it, made decisions, and kept things from spiralling out of control. They were the superstars, the rock gods, and the savvy leaders. I was certain they *knew* things that us younger folk weren't privy to. They must have to be in charge. Surely, the answers to all of life's largest questions were available to them. Right? And the elderly were just along for the ride. Having given up the reins before going into retirement.

I couldn't wait for my generation to take over. How would we run things when we were finally in charge? What decisions would we make and what improvements? Certainly, we could do better than the world as it was. I couldn't wait for our teen heart-throbs to become the headliners, and for our creative minds to put their high-tech skills to use. The adults to our young generation would then become our elderly, retired and watching us from the sidelines in awe.

ROTFL.

I was such a foolish child.

I hadn't realized that each 'era' is really a multiverse of generations, a quantum patchwork of timelines intermingling like microscopic galaxies in a petri dish. One age group doesn't really relinquish control to another—everyone is networked like a series of complex circuits on a motherboard. (How's that for twenty-first century imagery?)

If my generation was meant to be 'in charge' when we were classified as adults, how have I gone from feeling like an unprepared child to feeling obsolete? Because that is how I sometimes feel. I watch the video clips now on social media and reel from how quickly they go. There is so much talking *at* you in the shorthand of a new generation and all the things we understood life through are disappearing. Bye-bye television, radio, and print. I blinked and seem to have skipped the feeling-in-control part. I look around now and all the innovators and leaders look like babies. Is this what today's adults look like? Is this what happens when you're suddenly the same age as the A-list celebrities' parents? Are children just maturing faster or did we get put out to pasture before our time? And again, where was I when my generation was meant to be in charge? Was I too busy trying to figure out where I was at to actually *adult*? And if so, how did the others do it? Why couldn't I find a way to contribute to our imprint? Good Lord, does it always boil down to this question? What could I have done to be of relevance? To have been relevant instead of just watching life go by.

I blinked and what should have been magnificent became mundane.

I blinked and got stuck with only reruns on Netflix.

RANDOM NOTE

Life is mostly froth and bubble,
Two things stand as stone,
Kindness in another's trouble,
Courage in your own.

—Adam Lindsay Gordon

*An undated note to self

The Yes Zone

Gillian Anderson, the actor, was on my mind when I woke up this morning. She's been all over social media, having turned up for an awards show in Los Angeles wearing a controversial, if symbolic, gown. It was reportedly embossed with the female genitalia. A far cry from her days as the drably dressed Agent Scully on *The X-Files* . . . and looking nothing like the tiny, unassuming woman in front of me in a London coffee shop queue nearly thirty years ago. (Wait, let me catch my breath here—THIRTY YEARS AGO?! Good Lord . . .)

Anyway . . . Gillian Anderson, in line for coffee. Like me, she had just moved to London (albeit temporarily, it seemed then) to do a show on the West End. Or film a movie. Or some such other interesting, creative project. I was there to do my master's. My trajectory since has not quite been as stellar as hers. If one were to judge it by the number of award show invites received.

This early morning thought of the highly regarded actor led me down a rabbit hole of reminiscence. I recalled the name of that now closed coffee shop—AROMA—its exact location on Long Acre just steps from the Covent Garden tube station, and the bright primary colours of its mismatched dishes. It was my favourite place for a cuppa back then. Before I developed more *sophisticated* tastes in caffeine.

The coffee shop was tied to and housed in branches of a then popular bookstore chain—Books Etc—but this one in

Covent Garden was a stand-alone. As was the AROMA in the foyer of the Royal Festival Hall—but I digress.

Point is—this one mental snapshot of Gillian Anderson took me back three decades . . . and I didn't even realize the nostalgia dripping out of me until someone I spoke to about it said, 'You're clearly missing London.'

Before I could agree, they adjusted their statement: 'Or maybe you just missing being younger.' Ouch. But true. That morning, I had lain there mustering the energy to get up and face another day—and it was not easy. Like most mornings had become. My body ached (of course), my head throbbed from lack of sleep, and I could barely see the point of rising. (Are you seeing a pattern in this book?) Then, I had a momentary vision of what it was like waking up in London. When I was in my twenties. No aches or pains. No regrets about the kind of pillow my head was on or the way it arched my neck as I slept. No hangover too debilitating, no insomnia too taxing. Back when every morning seemed bursting with possibility and there was no predicting where the day would lead. Sometimes, it was to a surprisingly lovely walk along the river or a spontaneous night at the theatre. Maybe even both on the same day. There were unexpected afternoons in Portuguese family restaurants and thought-provoking art talks in museums, and unforgettable evenings making new friends in dark, smoky jazz clubs and at cutting-edge cultural events. There was learning about being 'shut-in' at pubs that closed to the public before midnight and getting an unplanned Wine & Spirit Education Trust qualification. Boredom couldn't exist because there was always something new to experience and explore. Everything seemed possible, and even when tinged with melancholy, there was always a hint of adventure around every corner.

Back then, no matter how seemingly strange the question, the answer was always yes. *Want to hop on the train to Paris this weekend?* Yes! *Game to check out the boat festival in Richmond later?* Yes! *A new Ethiopian place just opened—*yes! *There's a .99 pence promo for* Antony and Cleopatra *at the Globe, want to stand among a crowd in the stalls for four hours just like they did in Shakespeare's day?* Why yes! I'd love that! (It wasn't as fun as we'd hoped.) *Oh, Ralph Fiennes doing a reading of* The English Patient *at Borders?* Yes, yes, yes! And even when I was the one asking myself the questions—*Any interest in listening to Jean Baudrillard speak at the ICA—*yes! was an easy reply. All the yeses amounted to a breadth of soul expansion. I felt like the world was just waiting to show off its wonders and I was chomping at the bit to be dazzled by it. Even when I remember those days, the colours are more vivid than the scene currently outside my window—an overpopulated, putrid city in soft focus from smog, tinged in the hues of dehydrated urine.

But I think back to my decade in London . . . and catch my breath. Loud. Vibrant. *Open* despite the crowds. And endlessly crackling. Like the feeling of New Year's Eve—turned quotidian. If the jubilation of fireworks could be captured on a grid and city map—that would have been it. Yes, all that in my memories of London.

Looking back now, I realize it wasn't so much *living* in the capital of Cool Britannia that I miss—Lord knows someone in their twenties and thirties would lead a very different existence there to someone in their forties and fifties—but the feeling, the certainty, that life was full of surprises and anything was possible.

These days, I sometimes can't even see the road ahead for all the smog. If someone says: *Fancy dinner at—*I say no before they can even finish asking the question. *There's a new dance performance—*no. *So-and-so is in town—*no. *Up for . . .* no, no, no! I wake up tired and in so much pain that it sometimes hurts to breathe. As for sleep, forget about it. I barely get two hours in, and when I do, it is the sleep of the dreamless and fried. Frayed. Take your pick—either word works. And we all know that when there is no sleep, there is no space to recharge. So, I feel like I have been on a ceaseless wheel going nowhere for— oh, the last half decade. Since I quit my job. Since I decided I no longer wanted to be in the relentless profession I had been in since I was nineteen. After nearly three decades, hard stop—I decided to change course. But I didn't know what that might mean. Where that road might lead. There wasn't even really a road before me. Someone somewhere once said something about putting one foot in front of the other when you don't know where you're headed, well, I didn't even have the energy for that. I just knew I had to get off the ride I was on. Because my own life seemed to be whizzing past me in a blur. I didn't feel like I was *participating* in it—merely seeing it all go by. So, I paused and I tried to make do while I figured things out—dipped into savings, took on small projects here and there, and took a breath, a breath, a breath—wanting to give myself the space to reorient. To re-examine my options and my choices. Regrets? Maybe one or two . . . but not really. It is what it is, you know? I couldn't keep going—so I paused. I paused . . . and sort of feel like I got turned around. Lost and a tad confused. But I told myself the alternative—being tied to a job that was eating me alive—would have been worse.

So then, why do I feel like I've been dragged through the mud and am now trying to swim in quicksand?

#

Fast forward. It's another morning. Another new day. I was going about my errands, aka my daily drudgery, and found a coin on the side of the road. Obvs, I picked it up. Habit,

I suppose, or desperation. Maybe, fingers crossed, it would bring me good luck.

I have always been compelled to collect roadside coins—they add up. And suddenly, I feel like. . . **Yes,** *I got this!* I realized that I'd just forgotten that every day—every bloody day—we get to wake up is one that comes with the promise of miracles. Every day is a fresh start and a blank canvas. I may not be in my twenties, earning in pounds and living in London, heck, I may not even be in a location I like . . . but every morning, I can choose to have a good day or not. It is up to me to see the road ahead as one full of opportunities or obstacles. Ultimately, they're just two sides of the same coin.

Every new day should be met with the excitement that inherently comes with mornings—I have just forgotten how to see it.

Hot Chocolate and a Hermit

A new chocolate café has opened in my neighbourhood. It's owned and operated by local chocolate makers who have garnered international recognition for their products. Most things on the menu—bar maybe three items—have chocolate in them. From the savoury starters to the bread to the mains. Even the cocktails feature some form of cacao. In the last week, I have been twice—on the insistence of the people I was with. (And yes, I was actually social *twice* in a week!)

Anyway, so, the chocolate café. It's a popular spot. And with good reason. Every item I've tried there has been incredibly delectable, from the grilled chocolate sourdough bread to the masala spiced cauliflower 'steak' with chocolate balsamic reduction. Of course, the main attraction is the 70 per cent dark hot chocolate drink, made from owner's award-winning chocolate bars. This is not the thick, syrupy dipping chocolate of my youth. (Every morning, when we were children, hot chocolate would be made from actual cacao 'tablets' ground and melted in a pot of milk being heated on the stove. The consistency, when it was ready, was like molasses, and we would take pieces of sweet bread and dunk them in our cups. That was breakfast. Is it any wonder we all developed a sweet tooth?)

But the hot chocolate at this café was not the same wonderful sludge of my childhood. It was a runnier liquid that was clearly meant to be sipped. Warm and smooth, with an elegant flavour. It was a new experience. The first time drinking hot chocolate didn't throw me back to my childhood. I felt like a fancy pants having a post-meal drink somewhere in . . . say, Vienna. Why Vienna? I don't know—it just sounds fancy.

Fast-forward a few days, and here I was back in the chocolate café, this time for dinner with my cousin. The cosy, comfortable surroundings brought on a long rambling conversation where we spoke of everything from the mundane worries of our everyday—plumbers, electricians, the re-sanding of parquet floors, cleaners, dental appointments, and fibromyalgia—to our concerns about the future. As you might imagine, there was a **lot** to talk about. For different reasons, we had both been advised to abstain from chocolate for a while so neither of us could have a cup that evening. Yes, I know, silly to be at the chocolate café then, but heck, we couldn't help it. Being around cacao was enough to feel like we were enveloped in a warm blanket. We both seemed tired and weighed down, and perhaps being around all that chocolate—even if we couldn't indulge—gave us some form of comfort.

And that comfort extended to having the most open conversation with someone I have always been able to discuss the difficult questions with. So, after I told her all about Faye from Steps[2] talking about perimenopause on social media, she asked me how I envisioned my future. (This might seem like a leap, but it really wasn't.) *Envision the future?* The question made me think . . . and in that long pause, I realized I no longer saw one. A future. I suppose having both my parents die young made me unable to see past the ages they were at when they passed. I think subconsciously, it made me feel like I had an expiration date. And it was fast approaching. This inevitable end. It's very hard to ponder a future when you don't think you'll have one.

---

[2] See chapter entitled: *One Step* at a Time

I know I didn't feel like that when I was younger. Back when I first started working. I was still in my teens—gung-ho, gregarious, and filled with gumption. Somewhere along the way, I lost all three. Leaving me nothing but a shell of my former self. Or so I saw it. By then, more than two decades had passed and I was exhausted. I had run myself ragged because it's what I thought I had to do. That's *professionalism*, right? It got so I careened off a ledge and there was nothing left but to free fall. Does this sound familiar at all? Surely, I can't be the only one who has felt like this. I was so fried I had to just take a leave. And that turned into a sort of early/semi-retirement from my career in journalism. In my forties. Recounting all this to my cousin at the chocolate café, she was quick to point out how lucky I was to be able to reinvent myself at this age—without feeling out of touch.

'Fifty is no longer what it used to be,' she reminded me. 'And you're still *young* enough to start afresh.'

Easy for her to say, I thought, though really—full disclosure—we're the same age and sort of in the same position. But unlike her, I was really struggling with not knowing what I wanted to do next. I went from having a career to not having one. From reporting facts to fiction writing. From a job to a ... hobby? Let me tell you, the latter doesn't actually pay. So I best figure out something else to do to support this 'young enough to start afresh' stage. *What to do? What to do? What to do?* This question dominates my every sleepless hour—and I have yet to find any answers.

When I worked for CNN in London, I was sent out on a story to an estate that was reviving a trend from Georgian times. A form of employment that had long become obsolete. It was spring, gardens were in bloom, and this was an exercise in ... whimsy. It dated back to the 1700s, when English estates were shifting from large, symmetrical gardens that they remain known for to wilder, untamed landscapes that featured the 'irregularities' of nature. Everything from forests, mountains, a menagerie or two, and aviaries. Capping it off, as a sign of just how wealthy the owners were, they took to hiring hermits as part of the ornamentation. Yup, you read that right. A live hermit. Actual people were hired to sit around these gardens by themselves and . . . ruminate. They resided on the estate in spartan hermitages or caves, or any such space allotted to them by their employers. Their task was to bask in all that nature in solitary contemplation, and should there be guests, they were to wander around the estate offering thoughtful conversation. They did receive remuneration at the end of their contract, which could go from weeks to years. One article called them spiritual surrogates. Presumably because estate owners were too busy with things of this world to bother with more esoteric pursuits like meditating on the meaning of life. It can be likened to Catholics in the Middle Ages, who could basically pay the church to forgive their signs and assure them a path to heaven.

What a trip. Ornamental hermits. I couldn't believe I'd never heard of it. And there I was with a news crew about to witness a twenty-first century version. The said estate was doing it to attract tourists. And just like in Georgian times, they put an ad in the papers to find their hermit. (Yes, people still read printed papers in the early twenty-first century.)

He—the hermit—was a nice enough chap. Early thirties, if I recall correctly. Was in between jobs and needed some time to ponder his next steps. This was a perfect way to do that and earn some cash as well. He was dressed in brown, like a monk, and was staying in a cave on the estate for the duration of a weekend. By the end of it, he had hoped to have found some answers.

I don't know why that story came to mind. Maybe that's what I should be doing? I wonder if anyone on an English estate is in want of a hermit. Should I go find a cave somewhere and dress like a monk in brown? Oh, to be afforded such a luxury. Instead, there I was wearing blue in a chocolate café with my cousin, unable to drink the soothing liquid and seeing little past the darkness outside. I guess all the world is our untamed landscape, and our questions won't always be answered the way we expect. But hidden throughout, there are 'caves' and 'grottoes' for quiet contemplation—and even our expectations evolve with time.

So, there I sat in a chilly chocolate café in the middle of a bustling city, pondering what it was I could see in my future. As I surfed the waves and whirlpools of my emotions, my cousin waited . . . until I let the tide flip me onto my back to face the stars.

HAVE I CHANGED · · · AND HOW?

An Afternoon at the Power Station

It began with a lunch. A long-planned get-together with two other writers. We were new friends who clicked from the get-go and for months, had been trying to arrange another meet up. Despite none of us having a proper 9-to-5 job, we couldn't quite get our schedules in sync. We'd been busy, you see, pouring ourselves into our independent pursuits . . . or all tied up searching for what it was we should be pursuing.

Then, one dull, hopeless day at the start of a new year, things just sort of fell into place.

'See you at the Grid?' the most positive (and reclusive) of us exclaimed. It was more a statement than a question. Because, of course, where else would three empowered women meet for a meal? *Ahem.*

The Grid was the dolled-up food hall in an old power station that had been dolled up as a mall. At the Grid, we could all eat what we wanted without worrying that one among us was having to compromise on their meal. Well, wouldn't you know it—out of twenty-plus stalls, we all chose food from the same vendor. We laughed at the coincidence. But we should have seen it as a sign that we were in for an afternoon of synchronicities.

It had been a challenging year for all of us and we were in need of commiseration. The wisest of our trio—as evidenced by her peaceful countenance and the unabashed greys in her hair—began our exchange of woes. But at the end of every turn of her narrative, she chose a positive outlook. (If you've never heard a tragic tale get a happy ending, then maybe it's not being told right.)

'It's all good, yeah?' the wise one again posed a statement in the form of a question. 'It's all good.'

The way she saw it, no matter what occurred, it led to a necessary development that would in turn bring you where you needed to be. It wasn't about accomplishments or business goals or profit-making endeavours—life, as she saw it, was about following the signs around you 'from the Universe', trusting in a sort of Sacred Flow, letting go of the reins and enjoying the ride. I know it sounds overly simplistic and more than a tad ridiculous, especially for nay-sayers and those who like to think they're either in control or that nothing is. But what harm could there be in allowing what's joyful?

Our chatter went on for more than the two hours I had initially allotted for it. But I came out of it feeling much lighter than when I first sat down. Even though I hadn't necessarily shared what was weighing on me, the energy around the table was enough to lift my flagging spirits. So when the Wise One suggested a short walk to see her new abode, it was easy to agree.

'It just has such a wonderful energy, you know?' Again, a statement from her, not a question.

As I had already learned, when you say 'Yes'—good things can happen.

Before we got to the exit of this dolled-up power station, we ran into someone else who looked as lost as we'd felt earlier. She was a friend of the other two writers I was with and was on her way to a meeting when it was suddenly cancelled. She seemed stressed and in need of a hug. Not unlike the rest of us.

'We're off to see the Wise One's new place, wanna come?'

It sounded like an invitation to traipse down the Yellow Brick Road and see the Wizard.

The new 'recruit' looked at her mobile phone for barely a second, glanced at each of us for a tick, then, seemingly on instinct, jumped in to join the adventure.

It was as if Dorothy—the lost teen from L. Frank Baum's timeless and endlessly reinvented *The Wizard of Oz*—had picked up the equally lost lion, tin man, and scarecrow. In varying combinations of those characters' listlessness, fearfulness, and uncertainty. The crew for the Wise One's journey home was complete, and we followed her to what could easily have been an overhyped abode of Oz-level illusion and deception. Is this what people do when they feel lost and alone? Hope to find a tribe for company and solace?

Well, her place was wonderful. And though only half furnished, we made ourselves comfortable enough to stay well into evening. There was an old banyan tree in the garden, and we sat around a wooden table drinking tea. In such like-minded company, we managed to talk each other through our shadows. We laughed, we cried, we snacked and played some cards, like time had stopped and we were suspended in a sub-version of reality that we all needed.

Under the canopy of that sturdy banyan, we saw false idols for what they were and faced our fears.

On that one afternoon's *yeses* from the power station turned mall, I felt reinvigorated in a way I had thought no longer possible. I suddenly saw no obstacles to joy and felt free of any limitations. Simply because I gave myself permission to be lost . . . and took the time to pause.

I was reminded that when you trust the flow, things work out, and in that, we find the power not just to renew ourselves but each other.

Drafting 101

By now it's no secret that I enjoy writing. Not talking out loud or presenting or any other performative act. But putting down letters on a page. The physical craft of fashioning thoughts in alphabet. It's like doing a jigsaw puzzle but with words. When you put just the right sequence down, it can be magic. And other times . . . well, nowadays you can just relieve yourself of cack with a DELETE button.

Are there moments I wish I could press the delete button on and do over? I used to think not, but on later reflection—(and I mean <u>later</u> not *deeper*, because it isn't upon deeper or more profound introspection that I reached another conclusion, but a consequence of thinking about it again *later* in time)—maybe there are a few instances when I wish I had handled things differently. What gets me through the doubt is knowing that at every point I've had to make a decision, I did so according to my gut. Trusting my instincts and guided by my conscience. So, I suppose the only regret I might have is not having been wise enough to know better. I also wish I had been less afraid.

That's the biggest challenge really. Our own fears. They're like a straitjacket. Immobilizing and constricting. I got tired of being stagnant. And it was only later I realized we have the power to change the stories we tell ourselves about our lives.

Take, for example, people who up and move in their forties. Can you imagine the courage it takes to uproot oneself and relocate at an age that 'adults' were once expected to be *settled down*? To make changes at such a point when many others would think it too late to 'start afresh'? Imagine what it's like for those who begin a new journey in their fifties. Who change jobs. Shift interests. Accept failures and attempt something new. At fifty! Geez. There it is again—fifty—how the heck did this happen? Many of my friends have expressed the same sentiment: 'Fifty?! How the heck did this happen?'—word for word. I kid you not.

When we were in our thirties, looking at fifty seemed like gazing into oblivion. There was little beyond it other than time to slowly wind down our lives. But now that I am circling the rim of this oblivion, people are going on about how 'fifty is the new thirty', et cetera, et cetera. What a wonderful notion, but I call BS! You can *think* you are still thirty—but your knees will remind you otherwise. Or your digestive system. And that extra layer of fat you just can't shake. When people start to call you *ma'am* instead of *miss*, there is no denying you ain't a young filly no more. Or when you are offered the extra seat on the bus or in a room. Thank you, but WTF. (No really, thank you—I appreciate the offer, but I fear if I sit down, I will have trouble getting back on my feet.)

Again, I digress.

The other day I happened to chance upon my reflection—I think I stopped looking at mirrors some five years ago, when I left journalism and no longer had to face the TV cameras—and I gave myself such a fright. It was like seeing my mother look back at me. I think I was even wearing her duster and a pair of her spectacles that I had had re-lensed for my needs. *When did I turn into my mother?!* When did I slip into middle age? For some reason, this is the time frame in which I have preserved my late mother—when she was middle-aged. Except fifty isn't middle age when you pass away in your sixties, now is it?

Good Lord, my kingdom for a point! Where was I going with this? Ah yes, I think it was second chances? Of course, second chances. How it is never too late to *rewrite* your story.

That's what all the self-styled self-help gurus are saying, right? You can be 'middle-aged' or in your 'latter years' and yet start again. Well—*again*—I call BS.

Here's what I've learned: like a live news report, you **can't** rewrite your story, only <u>add</u> to it. Adjust it—adapt it—re-frame or re-shape it. But you can't delete everything you've just broadcast or lived through and start from zero. No matter what you might tell yourself. Truth is, life is all about learning to pivot. (Anyone else immediately think of that hit '90s show about six friends when they hear the word 'pivot'? Anyway . . .)

Pivot. That's what helps you get through any rough patch. Not letting yourself feel defeated or crushed but keeping your head lifted to keep searching for a way to get past or through whatever it is that might be proving challenging. Because there is always another way.

This is what I've gleaned from working in news for three decades, from meeting people during some of the most difficult days of their lives: Humanity, for the most part, is made up of survivors. People pivoting, constantly changing course, to get through any darkness and trauma in search of the sun.

This is what I **know** from decades of *scripting* news: you can visualize a story, organize your thoughts around an assignment and plan as much you like, but be ready to pivot. You never know what will come at you out of nowhere. And you can never be prepared enough for what's spontaneous. So, be observant. Be loose, and don't confine or lumber yourself with presumptions and preconceived notions—life is never what it seems. And the words we might use to describe our existences—to feign control over our reality and our dreams—they are only crutches, holding us back from greater truths that might be too frightening. We are leaning on signifiers, pointing to an eternal abyss where meaning resides.

Stuck and Flow

You can't escape it. Everything you try to flee in life will travel with you wherever you go. That heartache, the anger, the loneliness . . . the heartburn and the gas. You take it with you no matter how far you roam. Sure, a new location can shake things up and help you see differently, just as looking away from your laptop screen to a window will adjust your gaze. That momentary glance at a new horizon can make everything seem fresh and free—but that's only because you won't have any shadows or ghosts attached to it yet. At least none that will catch up with you in the initial days. But mark my words: they *will* come. They will come for you. You cannot escape your nightmares when you take your *self* with you wherever you go. So, best learn to grapple with your demons. To sit in silence with your discomfort and unease until they no longer have power over you. I always believe the best way to get over something is to just go through it. Denial, distraction, debate—none of that works. You can't deny yourself out of something or distract yourself from pain. And you can't win a debate with yourself unless you're willing to also throw up your hands in defeat. I say it's better to learn how to throw one's hands up in acceptance. Letting things in, looking at them, taking them apart, or staring them down does not mean submission or giving up—but it diminishes any hold they might have over you. Once you examine or get to know something—a fear, a person, a situation—it is no longer distant. No more a frightening stranger. And without the phantom, you are left with nothing but light.

The Golden Line

There's a guy online selling his supposed expertise in putting together résumés that will successfully get you employed in the current job market. He calls himself a certified résumé expert. Of course. Apparently, the substance of the information in your document may not matter as much as the way it is formatted. Yes, the layout and the choice of words are being used to rule out job applicants who come across as 'old'. Yup, he said old. Nothing to do with the date of your college graduation or when you started your first job—he used 2002 as an example of *too far back in the past to count!*—but if you so much as have this information listed in your résumé, it lets the prospective employer know that you are not of the much-desired digital generation. Hence, as far as said prospective employer is concerned, you've revealed yourself as unable to fill the role they have vacant. Not for a second might they consider that maybe the way they're looking to fill these roles is formulaic. *Sans* creativity. Actually, these days, it seems that's exactly what they want. As limitless as technology is making the world, we're making each other fit in boxes. Candidates have to tick certain criteria and use certain words to even get past an algorithmic filter or an applicant tracking system (ATS). A tracking system! But of course, an automated selection process. A *machine* has been trained, i.e., programmed, to choose candidates for a job via keywords and pre-defined details. The significance of our human experiences parsed down to a few strokes and symbols. And if we don't know the right code, then we don't pass muster. We are spent chaff deservedly separated from the grain. Well, FML.

According to this certified résumé expert, aside from learning to use the right words, you must not use dates in your list of previous employment or educational achievements. It could work against you, (example: 2002, as I mentioned up top). The bare facts and figures won't show employers or their recruiters if you are qualified for a job, but what will is *how* you present your accomplishments. So, drop the '1999—graduated with a master's degree' or whatever academic achievement, and definitely no dates of birth. (I hadn't even realized that was a thing. I wonder what the expert will say about me in response to that!)

What I gathered from this man's social media feed, which of course I checked out, is that résumés today have to read more like a dating profile. Job experience has to be whittled down to highlights and presented as colourful blurbs. Short and punchy to make the employer want to swipe right or left, whichever way means they want to meet you. Basically, you are a product that they should want to buy. And if you don't know how to sell yourself, then you're screwed.

So this certified expert was offering his skills as a kindly service to help the elderly, who, by his standards, meant everyone above forty-five. Forty-freakin'-five! Let me tell you—I wanted to reach into the phone and swipe that silly smile off his face. (Kidding.)

But really, this dude was offering to help people like me fight 'ageism' without realizing that the very way he presented it was ageist. Of course. You tell us we're old, then you cap that with saying we're undesirable in the job market? At forty-five? What makes these people think that someone born in the LATE twentieth century can't function in a meme and emoji world? We might hate it, but it doesn't mean we don't *get* it.

Ugh.

To be honest, seeing this certified expert's 'helpful' reels made me feel rather ancient. It's bad enough when people call you ma'am and treat you gingerly like you need help getting seated or when they smile politely and end conversations when you walk into a room. Wait, I've said this earlier, haven't I? (See? I am repeating myself too—Lord help my résumé!) But you get the picture.

Sidenote: I was once referred to as my sister's mother. It was horrific. (Horrific for me, my sister thought it was a gas.) I have convinced myself that the only reason the salesperson called me that is because my sister, who is barely four years younger than me, took my credit card to pay for a purchase. What the salesperson didn't realize was that my sister had tried her card in an earlier store and it wasn't working. So, she asked me to help out until her bank came back online. I have yet to live down that moment.

But really, making presumptions is crass and impolite. It's an imposition of your preconceived ideas on others. It used to be that people thought I had just given birth because I put on a few extra pounds but not enough to come across as actually pregnant. Now, they just come right out and ask if they can help me by suggesting a good diet! Thanks, but no.

I have veered off track again. My apologies. My point is, there are reminders enough everywhere that we—people 'forty-five and up'—are seen by many as 'old', but that doesn't mean we have outlived our purpose or lost our lust for life. (Never mind what several earlier chapters in this book might say!) So, please don't treat us like that. I have never looked to a person older than me and thought them incapacitated or in some way disadvantaged simply because of their chronological age. Dare I wonder what these 'youngsters' today might think of powerhouses like eighty-seven-year-old Jane Fonda and seventy-nine-year-old Dolly Parton? Or what their thoughts might be about trailblazing and culturally influential personalities like Shakira, Microsoft

CEO Satya Nadella, and the infamous Elon Musk? Gen X, Gen X, and Gen X. And certainly not old.

I know K-pop and anything Korean is big these days, but have you ever heard of *hwangap*? It's a Korean tradition where they celebrate someone turning sixty. The age of reckoning. Based on the sixty-year cycle of the lunar calendar traditionally followed in East Asia. A new cycle begins after turning sixty. Hwangap was once seen as a mark of longevity, but people are living longer these days and the celebration is now more about acknowledging that someone has earned the right to take on an advisory role in society. In short, they've been through a lot and they *know* things, so it would be wise to seek their counsel.

In Japan, where the same tradition is known as *kanreki*, turning sixty is not just a time to honour one's achievement but to look towards the future. It's literally seen as time of rebirth. Of reinvention. And that renaissance of self is often marked with a change of name. To be fair, Japan can be said to celebrate re-imaginings as a whole. Perhaps because the country itself has had to do it so many times throughout its history. Even its best-known artists from the period of its cultural isolation used different names at different stages of their creative evolution. But each time, no attempt was made to hide the original identity. It's no wonder then that they also have the art of *kintsugi*. You must've heard of this one—the craft of repairing broken pottery by applying gold (or silver, or platinum) dusted lacquer on the cracks. It's become such a powerful metaphor everywhere— even beyond Japan's borders—for resilience and transformation. For acceptance and finding beauty in 'imperfection'.

I wonder what Mr Certified Résumé Expert would have to say about that. Or does he perhaps think that that is what he is offering? The gold-dusted gum to hold together the pieces of our past in a way as to make us palatable to a machine helping a younger generation of employers?

Here's where a line must be drawn. A former bank teller might not seem suitable to manage a medic dispatch service because the keywords in his résumé will likely not match the job description. But the ex-teller could very well be hyper-organized, quick to learn, and handle pressure well enough to be able to effectively dispatch response teams. And what if he were just the right person to hold the department together? A machine would have ruled him out if he didn't know how to frame himself right for the ATS.

Don't we all need to be able to step outside our pre-defined boxes? Especially when it comes to finding work. To determining what it is that we will spend a huge chunk of our time *doing*.

I just read an article about all these people who 'didn't find success' until later in life. Success being defined as professional recognition. Many of them went through several cycles of reinvention before landing on something that worked. And yes, it gave me hope that maybe there is no deadline to 'finding another dream'. That perhaps this is my period of kintsugi. When I myself must learn to appreciate the cracks for my own metamorphosis.

Here is what I am learning: there is no finish line to transformation, only continuous cycles of transition that will lead to—fingers crossed—a golden era.

RANDOM NOTE

Forty is the old age of youth.
Fifty is the youth of old age.

—Victor Hugo

Level 50

So, I think I have hit a new level of maturity. I say new because I have not felt quite like this before. I woke up today with no pain . . . and nothing gnawing at me. No upset that I was dreading facing.

The sun was out . . . the breeze was cool . . . and I had a good cup of coffee after I did some t'ai chi.

Today, for the first time in a long time, I felt like myself. Just . . . a person. Enjoying where she was at. Not *wanting* anything nor *fearing* anything nor anxious about needing to get something done. I went for a walk . . . and just looked at everything that was new in the neighbourhood . . . and it felt like the world was wide open. I didn't feel too old or too young for any of it. I just . . . was. Even better, no one could offend me or cause me upset—because I found I just didn't care. What others might think no longer affects how I move through life. I make no excuses for who I am nor do I expect them from you. And I respect the right to privacy. Mine and yours. There are things that do not need to be shared.

Despite the rules imposed on us, we all live by our own, and we should only fight the battles we choose. Unfortunately, this is still a world where many people are forced into situations they would rather not be in—poverty, injustice, abuse—who in their right mind would choose that but the perpetrator? I don't mean to get on a soap box but oh how I wish those who *can* would do more to help those that can't. Oh! There it is—a wish.

Perhaps, somehow, there are things that I can *wish* for again. That I can strive to be part of.

Do I want to be part of something again? A question I am honestly asking myself. I have a friend who's a counsellor and she's always reminding people that life isn't all about *doing*. That we are not here to 'accomplish' things and there are periods when it is enough to just *be*. That we should learn to allow for the silences or the chaos and be all right with either. She has just turned sixty. And I have never seen her happier.

As I near the stage between fifty-plus-year-old Jennifer Aniston and nearly ninety-year-old Judi Dench, I realize that *maybe* I no longer feel so old? As I said earlier, fifty-year-old Bea Arthur is a far cry from a fifty-year-old Sarah Jessica Parker. Our definitions of youth and age, like life, are not set in stone. And they've clearly *transitioned*. So I best get in the right frame of mind to enjoy the ride. My joints might hurt and my back may ache, but I guess I should see that as a call to exercise. There are women close to seventy who can still show off their abs! But more than that, a strong core has enabled them to do more things and move through the world with less or non-existent pain. #Goalzz

Speaking of abs, in 2023, eighty-something-year-old actor Robert De Niro and his thirty-something-year-old partner had a baby. (Yes, I know, tenuous connection, but an effective line transition nonetheless, wouldn't you say? Ahem.) Anyway, it remains a terribly controversial development. Critics say it was selfish of him to have become a father at such a late age when he must know he can't possibly be around long enough to raise the child. But these days, late is relative, and every second De Niro *is* around is more than the time given by countless deadbeat folks who walk away from their children. No matter what age they're at. No?

Around the same time, fifty-plus-year-old actress Sofia Vergara ended her marriage because her husband wanted children and she didn't want to be an 'old' mom. Which also makes sense. She may want other things at this stage of her life, or she may just be too tired. Whatever her reason—which is really none of our business—women undoubtedly have a more pronounced (understatement) biological change to deal with when they hit a certain age. Talk about marking a transition. Aside from physical pain and discomfort, we also have to learn to ride the turbulent waves of our emotions, as we question who we are and everything around us. Like bloody teenagers all over again, only worse. It's like getting on a wild horse before he's broken in. And do you then choose to 'medicate' the animal—or not?

So many questions. And frankly, at the end of the day, who are we to judge anyone else's choices? With regard to the aforementioned actors, if anything, their decisions should inspire us to make the most of the time we have. However we might choose to do so. Why should we curtail our exuberance for life or temper it based on chronological age? Why should we be afraid to want the things we want because we fear we might be too old?

#

My cousin just passed away. It has struck me deeply. She was barely in her forties. A warm, wonderful woman with two small children and the most amazing husband. It still feels weird to me to call her a woman. She was always and will remain the vivacious young girl I'm now preparing to tuck away in my memory. She had such a zest for living, down to the last days of her radiation treatment . . . and into palliative care. And always, always, she managed to stay positive. So much so that I really can't believe she is gone. She was such a light, and her energy still shines so brightly. In the face of such grace, I am filled with shame. How dare I even pose a single existential question? I am here, as are you—and that is a *gift*. How dare I look a gift horse in the mouth? Enough.

Enough.

More and more I am running out of patience for melancholy. I know this isn't easy when someone is in the midst of a depression or indeed a 'crisis'. I apologize. But I have reached a stage when even my own malaise feels like a waste of time. I *know* there are better ways I can spend my energy than on ennui. And the fact that I can even write this reminds me how lucky I am. I have been able to sit with my sadness and my uncertainty and ponder, ponder, ponder. I have been able to write and let things go with the stroke of a pen. I will keep learning, I have survived, and I will carry on. Because . . . be-cause . . . *be,* cause.

I read somewhere that people are now referring to their chronological age as if it were a level in a game. Makes it more palatable by inferring accomplishment. It indicates how many rounds you've completed by triumphing over adversities. So a thirty-year-old is now at Level 30, a forty-year-old at Level 40. Et cetera, et cetera. Thinking of it like that makes it all less daunting.

The level I am at sees me *independently employed,* the *senior supervisor* of my time, and *executive producing* my morning at a local café. I am just now finishing the last of another glorious flat white. A warm chocolate chip cookie is sitting next to it, waiting to be devoured.

Sun, sun, sun, here we come . . . has just come over the speaker . . . indicating it is time to meet a new day.

RANDOM NOTE

We are not our age,
we are our energy.

* Various independent life coaches
** An actual occupation in the twenty-first century

Yet Another List

Things to be grateful for:

- Being alive . . . still
- A chance at reinvention
- You

BIG QUESTION #593

WHAT NEXT?

Acknowledgements

Building on the acknowledgements in my previous work, I would like to take this opportunity to express my gratitude to and admiration for a few more incredibly strong women who have all in one way or another contributed to this book.

Miriam Campa
Almudena Pfitz
Elena Montero
Georgina Arando
Iciar Weber
Mai Dillon
Sara McClintock
Cathie de Leon
Katherine Visconti

My thanks as well to the PRH SEA team who brought this book before you:

Nora Nazerene Abu Bakar, for bringing me into the family, Sneha Bhagwat and Adviata Vats, for their support and enthusiasm, and to Thatchaayanie Renganathan, who has edited all four of my books thus far, thank you for your invaluable insight and commitment to staying true to the author's voice.